Ethno-Nationalism in India

Interdisciplinary Perspectives

Edited by

Debajyoti Biswas

ATLANTIC

PUBLISHERS & DISTRIBUTORS (P) LTD

Published by
ATLANTIC
PUBLISHERS & DISTRIBUTORS (P) LTD
7/22, Ansari Road, Darya Ganj, New Delhi-110002
Phones : +91-11-40775252, 40775214, 23273880, 23275880
Fax: +91-11-23285873
Web: www.atlanticbooks.com
E-mail: orders@atlanticbooks.com

Printed & bound in India by Atlantic Print Services

Preface

The present endeavor is an anthology of eleven peer-reviewed research papers which had been presented at an International conference held at Bodoland University, along with an introduction. It interrogates the rise of ethno-nationalism in India with specific reference to Northeast India. It aims to bring interdisciplinary perspectives drawn from studies of culture, history, literature, and politics to the analysis of emerging areas of nationalism in India. In particular, it examines the ways in which literary-textual representations intervene in debates regarding ethno-nationalism, sub-nationalism, and other permutations of Indian nationalism. It examines a variety of political movements and literary works by various writers over the past five decades that have created, enshrined, and contested ideas pivotal to the rise of Indian nationalism.

The papers have been contributed by mid-career academicians and young researchers who have argued about the pros and cons of rising ethno-national consciousness vis-à-vis Indian nationalism. Most of the papers investigate into the causes that have catapulted the rise of ethno-nationalism in India. This is not a new phenomenon however, because there have been precedence of linguistic nationalism since the time of India's Independence. Once the first instance of balkanisation is set, it became a trend for smaller communities to seek recognition on the basis of language or ethnicity. Most of the papers in this volume deal with such stories of ethno-nationalism that resulted into the balkanisation of Northeast India. Seen from the perspective of the ethnic communities, their appeal for recognition or autonomy within the nation in the form of separate state is based on the issues of immigration, resource extraction, and development. However, there is another aspect to it. In a post-colonial nation-state like India, it is not possible to reverse the effect of immigration without depriving one or the other groups of their legitimate rights. Whereas the inflow of immigration to Northeast India was facilitated by the colonisers at first and then by the partition of India, the exodus of many of these immigrants has been affected by the violence of ethno-nationalism. Even after India's independence when the immigration continued unabated, it caused serious problems involving the local communities of the places where people migrated. This also hampered the interest of the early migrants and as a result any effective measure to protect them resulted in the loss of life and home. Homelessness is a trope in the literary works coming from Northeast India. This portends to the lackadaisical handling of the issues and a lack of clear cut policy to protect the ethnic-communities on one hand and to safeguard the legitimate victims of India's partition. This book addresses some of these issues. The book is only introductory in nature that familiarises the readers with the issues related to ethno-nationalism.

Debajyoti Biswas

Contents

List of Contributors

Debajyoti Biswas (Ph.D.) is an Assistant Professor of English at Bodoland University. He completed his MA in English from Jawaharlal Nehru University in 2003 and earned his doctorate from Gauhati University in 2017. He has completed two Minor Research Projects funded by University Grants Commission (UGC). His areas of interest include Anglophone writings from Northeast India, Nationalism and Identity Politics, Ecocriticism, Indian Writing in English and Critical Theory. He has contributed more than thirty articles in edited books and research journals. His articles have been published in international journals like *Corvinus Journal of Sociology and Social Policy* (Corvinus University of Budapest, Hungary), *RUDN Journal of Studies in Literature and Journalism* (RUDN University, Russia), *Policing: A Journal of Policy and Practice* (Oxford University Press), *Humanities and Social Sciences Communications* (Springer Nature) and *English: Journal of the English Association* (Oxford University Press). His co-edited book *Nationalism in India: Texts and Contexts* has been published by Routledge in 2021. His co-edited book *Global Perspectives on Nationalism: Political and Literary Discourses* is forthcoming from Routledge.

Ankita Baruah (Ph.D.) teaches Political Science in Assam Women's University, Assam. Her areas of interest are contemporary politics, political theory, women studies, gender issues, and feminism. She completed her doctoral on Social Exclusion of Women in Assam from Dibrugarh University. She has a number of research papers to her credit in reputed journals.

Debabhuson Borah (Ph.D.) is an Assistant Professor of English at Majuli College, Assam. He is a literary critic and researcher. He did his M. Phil on Chinua Achebe's novels and Ph.D. on Inter-textuality and Modern Assamese poetry from Gauhati University. He was awarded the prestigious Munin Borkotoky Literary Award in 2018 for his book Nirbachan. He has a number of publications in reputed journals. He represented Assamese language and literature several times in various conferences of Sahitya Akademi.

Parvin Sultana is currently working as an Assistant Professor at Pramathesh Barua College. Her research interests include gender, migration, minority, and politics. She has written research papers and book reviews for journals like *Social Change* (SAGE), the Book Review Journal, South Asia Journal, etc. Her research papers have been published in journals like *Meridian Critic Journal, Journal of Identity and Migration Studies, Policing* (OUP), etc. She also writes regularly for newspapers, webzines, and magazines both in English and in vernacular. Apart from teaching, she also works with the community in spreading awareness about girl education and women's rights in far flung areas of Assam.

Konkumoni Boro is a Ph.D. research scholar at the department of Humanities and Social Sciences, IIT Guwahati. Her major research interest lies in border studies, migration studies, citizenship, identity construction, and stateless communities.

Anuradha Nongmaithem (Ph.D.) is currently working as an Assistant Professor of English at the National Institute of Technology, Agartala. She is a keen lover of Manipuri literature, culture, dance, and customs. She is sensitive towards the downtrodden and a staunch feminist, who believes that every individual is equal. She has written more the 32 articles and also contributed chapters in several edited book and has presented papers in National and International seminars and conferences. She has two books to her credit. She is currently working on compiling her unpublished poetry collections for publication.

Apurba Borbora is a Research Scholar at the Department of English, Gauhati University. She has also served as an Assistant Professor in Sonari Commerce College, Charaideo, Assam.

Urbashi Borbora is a research scholar at the Department of English, Tezpur University. She has also served as an Assistant Professor at Sepon College. Her areas of interest are ELT, Linguistics, and Northeast Indian Literature.

Arun Nath is presently working as an Assistant Professor at the Department of English, Bodofa U.N. Brahma College, Dotma, Kokrajhar. His areas of interest are Indian English Literature, Post-colonial Literature, and Literature of Social Realism.

Doyir Ete (Ph.D.) is an Assistant Professor in the Department of English, Rajiv Gandhi University, Arunachal Pradesh, and specializes in Indian Writing in English, Diaspora Studies, Women's Writing, and North-East Writing in English.

Laki Molla is an Assistant Professor at the Department of English, Bhairab Ganguly College, Kolkata, West Bengal.

Krishanu Ghosh is an Assistant Professor at the Department of History, Bhairab Ganguly College, Kolkata, West Bengal.

Satya Nath Pegu is an Assistant Professor of English at Jengraimukh College, Majuli, Assam.

Tarulata Pegu is a Ph.D. research scholar at Assam University, Assam.

Manash Pratim Nath is a Junior Research Fellow (JRF) at Special Center for the Study of North East India, Jawaharlal Nehru University. His areas of interest include Carnivalesque, Indian Writings in English, Identity Politics and Nationalism, Northeast India, and Postcolonial Theory.

1

An Introduction to Ethno-Nationalism in India

Debajyoti Biswas

Modern nationalism that percolated into India during the freedom struggle was conditioned by European nationalism. Whereas modernity played an important role in moulding the social and political structure of modern India, the national consciousness was shaped by the urge to have the right of self-determination and self-rule. It would be erroneous to claim that national consciousness did not exist before nineteenth century, however, the consciousness of political unity along with territorial integrity over a vast stretch of land and the role of democracy in determining that nation came to be realised only from nineteenth century onwards. India has housed multi-ethnic communities and has over two hundred different languages and dialects. Along with various caste systems, there exists a class consciousness and strong religious sentiment among the inhabitants. With this diversity, it is a challenging task to talk of a national consciousness which is monolithic. However, the nationalism that emerged during the early nineteenth century saw the unity that foreshadowed the narrow class, caste, and religious differences. The growth of Indian nationalism then was propelled by the ambition to free India from British raj. As time went by, the parochial and self-limiting tendency of nationalism started cropping up like hydra's head and the fissure appeared in the form of religious nationalism. As a result, the country witnessed partition in 1947. Post-1947 things turned worse with the rise of linguistic and ethnic nationalism. The very model of nationalism that India emulated became a self-defeating formula because every ethnic group and every linguistic group started conceiving themselves as a separate nation. Consequently, the states were balkanised and new states based on language came into existence. The inclusive Indian nationalism came to be challenged by partisan powers who could not see beyond their narrow benefit and pushed India into a tumultuous phase of internal strife.

This struggle for micro-identities came into direct confrontation with the larger Indian identity resulting into inter-ethnic conflicts on one hand and conflict against the state as well. The impact of such conflicts is reflected in the social and political life of the people inhabiting in those strife-torn regions. For instance, the north-east India is one such troubled periphery that has seen not only balkanisation of the region based on linguistic and ethnic identity, but also ethnic cleansing of various communities from time to time. All this also find an expression in the literary works produced in India, where the writers articulate about the prospects and challenges faced by the communities in realistic terms. This volume intends to bring together articles that deal with ethno-nationalism in India with particular focus on India's north-east. The articles take into account the political movements, the social movements and their representation in literature.

The first article examines the rise of ethnic nationalism in India's north-east due to the onset of massive immigration during colonial rule which continued unabated till 1970s. The rise in immigrant population has proportionately stimulated the rise in ethnic violence in the region so much so that the Indian Government has to enact Armed Forces Special Powers Act to maintain peace in the entire region. The agitation against outsiders and foreigners culminated into the inter-ethnic conflicts resulting into balkanisation of north-east India as well. The writer examines the history of immigration in the context of Assam and gives us a perspective on how political parties, students' organisations and indigenous people gradually became involved in shaping the ethno-national identities of the people over a period of time. The authors maintain that Ambikagiri

Raichoudhury's (1885-1976) idea of the Assamese nation as '*jati*' in relation to the notion of India as a '*mahajati*' perhaps commenced the discourse of Assamese nationalism in a fresh light. The current issues on Assamese nationalism generally explain the discord between the civic and ethnic variants of nationalism defined by a common language, inheritance, and culture of the Assamese-speaking people. Several scholars, however, opine that 'Assamese nationalism' was instrumental behind the Assam Movement (1979-85). Significantly, the growth of Assamese nationalism has a connection with different phases of migration into Assam. The Assam movement demanded to identify and push back illegal immigrants and provide constitutional, legislative, and administrative safeguards to the indigenous Assamese people. Assam witnessed a number of violent cases such as Nellie massacre, along with the death of 855 activists, during long period of the movement. Though the movement ended formally on August 15, 1985 following the Assam Accord, its memory and consequences still preoccupy people of Assam in different ways. At the same time, juxtaposing 'nationalism' to the 'Assamese' in a simplistic way, of late, is not beyond trouble. This article examines the rise of Assamese nationalism in context of the Assam movement.

Sultana's essay *Nationalism and Minority Politics in Assam: A Look at AIUDF's Performance* examines the rise of regional political parties as a counter to national parties. The emergence of new political parties is seen as an offshoot of religious underpinnings in promoting the aspiration of particular ethnic groups. The author takes into account the role played by the Muslim electorates in the electoral politics of Assam. Muslims in Assam comprise one-third of its population. The community is electorally relevant and has often played the deciding factor in electoral outcome in a large number of constituencies. If one looks at the electoral outcomes over the period of time, it becomes very clear that Muslims have never voted en masse. They have historically voted for the Congress, the Left parties and even the Asom Gana Parishad. If one looks at the Muslims of Assam, two trends become obvious—on the cultural front, Muslims of Brahmaputra Valley have always emphasised on assimilation with the greater Assamese identity. But on the political front the community has time and again tried to reassert its stand on different issues. This assertion took various forms. While the experimentation with a political assertion started with East India Muslims Association (EIMA) and found a fuller expression with the formation of the United Minorities Front (UMF), these were short-lived experiments. The community was seen to enjoy some kind of political agency with the formation of the All India United Democratic Front (AIUDF) in the year 2005. However, the performance of AIUDF over the years has not been consistent. This article will try to understand the political expression of the community through the performance of AIUDF electorally and their stands on issues of national importance for Assam like illegal immigration, condition of minorities, national register of citizens, etc. In a political climate where the rhetoric of illegal immigration always occupies the centre stage, it is interesting to see that how the immigrant population allies with different political groups depending on the geographical locations.

The next chapter examines the struggle of another ethnic community which has been pushed out of their original homeland. The ethnic group called Chakmas inhabited the areas that are now been included in Bangladesh. Once uprooted this community till date tries to negotiate with their new identity and issues related to citizenship in their new homeland. The history of citizenship has been a struggle over how citizenship is to be defined and who should be included and who should be not. This makes citizenship not only highly contested but a constantly changing institution. While citizenship is often professed in terms of legal status, having a national identity as a member of a nation state, but citizenship is not confined to that alone. As the liberal nation-state model gets more complicated when immigrants of different nationalities enter the territory of a state. In recent decades, global developments have questioned the relevance of the state and its borders. It has been observed that with increased international mobility, the traditional nation-state boundaries has been increasingly challenged, where one may claim for transnational, extraterritorial, dual and post-national citizenship. It is against this backdrop, the article explores the construction and negotiation of identity and membership of a community that was pushed out of one territory in the pursuit of creation of homogenous nations in the wake of modern state building process. The Chakmas make continuous efforts to determine their status, identity, space, and homeland. This article investigates identity construction of the Chakmas across borders and also within the borders of the host state and their claims for citizenship. The Chakmas, original inhabitants of Chittagong Hill Tracts, migrated to India from East Pakistan due to religious atrocities and submergence of their land because of the construction of Kaptai Hydel Dam. Using in-depth fieldwork, the article analyses the case of Chakmas in India's north-east.

Anuradha Nongmaithem's article "The Role of Maibi in Safeguarding the Tradition of Manipur" deals with the role of women in safeguarding the regional tradition and its importance in nation-building. It also highlights the customs, tradition with special reference to the role of women in Manipuri society. India is a land of a diverse region, culture, and customs and together with this diversity, the umbrella term one nation called India exists. There is a colossal difference from one region to another. In today's scenario, the idea of nationalism is changing day by day due to the influence of a strong wave of globalization. Keeping the influence of globalization as the backdrop, the article focuses on how the *maibi* (shaman/sorceress) are safeguarding the culture, tradition, and custom of Manipur. Though national identity is a collective consciousness, the article highlights the importance of the indigenous way of life along with nation building process. The maibis are closely connected with the natural element and are a medium of connecting the people of Manipur especially the Meiteis to the past and future. Lai Haraoba is an important ritual festival of the Meitei community re-enacting the creation of the universe. The maibi dance forms symbolize certain essential moments in the formation and vitalization of the cosmic order. Women, especially in Manipur, have a unique role in terms of not only in religion but also in socio-economic development. The article vindicates the importance of preserving ones' traditions and customs which was passed on from one generation to another and how ultimately with its distinctive features Manipur amalgamate itself into becoming an Indian. Therefore, the article argues that how a regional and ethnic identity is sustained without compromising on the arching Indian national identity.

The next article engages the discourse on nationalism through the prism of literary text. The literary texts mirror the society in many ways including the social strife. In the twenty-first century, the fictional world realistically portrays the pressing concerns about one's identity and social relations. As such it has also come to address the issue of nationalism. Nationalism as an ideology can be pre-dominantly inclusive or exclusive. In a highly differentiated society, inclusiveness is indeed a process which takes place politically through common struggles, socially by overcoming internal social barriers and culturally by identifying a common past and invoking indigenous cultural consciousness. In India, the obstacles for achieving inclusiveness are social and not political—it is the problem of communal differences. There have been many riots, clashes, upheavals for ethnic, racial, and religious cause in post-Independent India which finds mention in the Anglophone fiction as well. Similarly, the writers from north-east India such as Easterine Kire, Temsula Ao, Arupa Patangia Kalita have narrated stories related to insurgency and communal clashes caused by ethnic nationalism. The characters in these works opt to deconstruct history—the history of conflict—to forgive and survive. This essay addresses the idea of inclusive nationalism by analyzing Easterine Kire's *Bitter Wormwood* and Arupa Patangia Kalita's *Felanee*. *Bitter Wormwood* especially narrates about the ordinary people who suffered during the Naga freedom struggle, rather than about its leaders and heroes. The novel *Felanee* encompasses the fortunes of displaced women of different ethnicities who are subjected to an atmosphere of fear and violence caused by the ethno-nationalist elements in Assam of the 1960s, 70s, and 80s. The characters Neibou and Felanee, having faced the horrifying consequences of ethnic and communal conflict, ultimately realize the necessity to overcome internal social barriers for a peaceful living. They project the need for an all-inclusive nationalism, achieved socially. The essay mainly aims to prove the importance of social aspect of inclusive nationalism which stands against ethno-nationalism.

Nationalism and Social Realism in Tabish Khair's 'Filming: A Love Story' by Arun Nath strongly articulates the rise of Indian nationalism after India's independence. Nationalism *is an ideology and movement characterized by the promotion of the interests of a particular nation, especially with the aim of gaining and maintaining the nation's* sovereignty or self-governance over its homeland. Nationalism holds that each nation should govern itself, free from outside interference, that a nation is a natural and ideal basis for a polity, and that the nation is the only rightful source of social and political power. This feeling aims to build and maintain a single national identity sharing social characteristics such as culture, language, religion and politics that promote national unity. Social Realism as a literary movement begins in France with the writings of Gustave Flaubert (1821-80) and Honoré de Balzac (1799-1850). Their writings were sustained in England through the novels of George Eliot (1819-80), and it was also introduced in the United States of America by the writings of William Dean Howell (1837-1920). Thus, the Social Realism in literature spreads worldwide in accordance with the need of the contemporary period. The essay focuses on Reconfiguring Nationalism and Social Realism in Tabish Khair's novel *Filming: A Love Story*. This novel is set primarily in India and spanning the twentieth century. It focuses on social and historical events like partition, the assassination of Mahatma Gandhi, the rise of photography and Bombay film industry, as well as the development of barbed wire with the everyday moments that make up the fabric of our lives. This article enumerates some of the basic tenets of Social Realism and Nationalism Theory, viz. racism, class struggle, immigration, cultural issues, humanism, identity crisis, and social anxiety which focus on some social welfare and human issues to analyze Tabish Khair's *Filming: A Love Story* as a social realism treatise.

Doyir Ete's essay deals with the plight of Chinese immigrant society who lived in India. The essay analyzes the space occupied by the immigrant Chinese community in India and how they negotiate their daily lives within the complex terrain of the nation. The Indian-Chinese have been living in India since the 1700s and through the centuries the community has undergone multiple experiences ranging from peaceful coexistence, to state victimization and incarceration, to a silent resistance and subsequent statelessness and dislocation. The author explores this interstitial space and encapsulates the conditions that problmatize the group's relationship with the Indian state. Within this historical framework, the author examines Kwai-Yun Li's *The Palm Leaf Fan and Other Stories* (2006) which is a first person account of the intricate and turbulent journey of the community in India. The author further explores the theme by engaging Rita Chaudhury's *Chinatown Days* (2018) which also narrates the history of the Chinese settled in Assam and their experience particularly during the Indo-China war of 1962. These stories envisage a space where multiple issues of identity and politics of the Indian-Chinese and its minoritarian position is foregrounded. These stories also raise pertinent questions like, how do the Chinese locate themselves in India? How should a nation/state like India respond to the narratives from these minority communities? And how should one respond to the predicament and ambivalence that is inherent in their narratives? The essay attempts to answer such questions through the stories of the community.

The next article examines the question of nationalism through subaltern perspective. The tribal—the indigenous people of India had a number of resistance movements and revolts against the colonial masters and they also laid down their lives for the sake of the country. But the mainstream nationalist historiography always ignored the contribution of the tribal and their movements and their leaders were never given adequate importance. Besides disrupting the hegemonic discourse of a homogenous and holistic nationalism, this denying by the mainstream historians is a lack in the 'original' narrative of a nation. The writers of the Subaltern Studies group challenged the theories of the dominant historiography by inscribing the histories of the marginal. Covering a period of ten years from 1967 to 1977 in Naxalbari region in the north of Bengal, Mahasweta Devi's *Bhasai Tudu* narrates the story of the agrarian revolution of the landless laborers against the oppressions of the *jotedar*, *mahajan*, *zamindar*, police and local bureaucracy. The firm and unambiguous political stand of the protagonist, who kept the revolution awake by rising from extermination, not fewer than five times, is a story of pride for any nation. But the heroism of these heroes goes largely unsung. On the other hand, these acts are presented in a negative light only to emphasize the huge gap that the tribal have with the mainstream people who uses them at their necessity. Through a close textual analysis, the essay points out the factors—both political and social that emphasize the difference between the mainstream people who have 'everything' and the tribal who have 'nothing'. The essay further explores, using Homi Bhabha's theory of 'liminality', how Mahasweta Devi, in writing the nation, focuses on the 'split' between the 'pedagogical' and the 'performative' and lays out the actions of Bhasai Tudu in the liminal space of the 'in-between'.

Satya Nath Pegu's essay examines how violence and oppression are invariably related to the growth of nationalism. The rise of jingoism and xenophobia has been witnessed in certain hyper-nationalisms in Germany, Italy, and Pakistan as well. Such nationalism is detrimental to peaceful coexistence and cultural assimilation. Nationalism is a sentiment of unity among a set of people occupying a particular territory, born out of common factors such as language, religion, economy, and administrative system. Nationalism, when it becomes synonymous with pure patriotism will prove a unique blessing to humanity and to the world but at the same time, it can also be terrifying and a hurdle to the universal civilization as it glorifies its own nation, stands for unity and solidarity of its own nation and leads to hatred of other countries. Nationalism makes people self-confined. They generally talk in terms of their own nation only. Nationalism also gives rise to imperialism; a source of continued violence and oppression. As scholars of nationalism from different schools of thoughts have argued, the conception of a nation and construction of national identity are inexorably related to a people's imagining of their history. History is a significant influence on their nationalism and patriotism. There is an obvious sense in which nationalist mobilization has an important basis in images of the past—images which are typically embellished to produce a tendentious image of the community's own history. Individuals are misinformed about their national history, and official narratives and propaganda frequently mischaracterize it. Pegu in his essay tries to trace out the distorted history and the influence of nationalism in Birendra Kumar Bhattacharya's *Love in the Time of Insurgency* (1960) and Gabriel Garcia Marquez's *One Hundred Years of Solitude* (1967). He attempts to bring out the political strategies such as violence and oppression in the select novels that is underscored by sentiments of nationalism.

Tarulata Pegu's *Oscillating between House and Home in Jhumpa Lahiri's 'The Namesake'* problematises the idea of house and home in the context of nation. The essay explores how house and home are creator and destroyer of identity for different characters. Pegu examines Jhumpa Lahiri's novel *The Namesake* (2003), to talk about the diasporic experiences of characters who immigrate and settle down in a new home away from homeland. It emphasizes how in one way or the other, the Indian Bengali identity and the feeling of nationalism are entwined even in a new setup. The study also sets to explore how certain individuals try to reinstate their old home with all the cultures and rituals intact to it and the difficulty faced by them in doing so. A formation of new identity out of amalgamation of two cultures is seen in the process. Home is invested with its irresistible power that pulls back the characters in right time. The essay concludes by stating how home serves both as a comfort and confinement for different characters and how they oscillate between house and home in search of freedom and happiness.

In the concluding chapter Manash Pratim Nath discusses about the very less talked about Kamatapur ethnonationalism. Whereas the once very powerful Koch Kingdom has ruled much of the lower Brahmaputra valley and many parts of Bengal and present day Bangladesh, their power gradually weaned away with the rise of Mughal Empire in India. The members of this community have been trying to claim their ethnic rights and tribal status for long along. They are also rightfully demanding a territory of their own where they can democratically govern and preserve their culture, language and religion. The Koch-Rajbangsis have a very chequered history owing to internal dispute and split in ethnic identity. This article proposes an inquiry into the circumstances that led to the rise in Kamatapur nationalism at the turn of the 20th century. In what could be described as a movement by the Rajbanshi people to give voice to their aspirations, the initial caste movement was inherently exclusionary, though in time the development of a language based Kamatapuri movement sought to include all those who spoke the Kamatapuri language. This chapter seeks to understand and explicate the circumstances, the divergent narratives and the process that went into the making of the larger inclusive Kamatapur movement. The movement must also be viewed in terms of its present context and other neighbouring sub-nationalistic narratives vis-à-vis the Assamese language movement.

The rise of ethno-nationalism as evinced from the above discussion points out the role of ethnicity, race, language, religion and culture as determinant factors. There is no single marker that can operate as centre of association when it comes to the politics of nationalism. If one delves back to the history of Assamese nation, it can be noticed that the Koch king Naranarayan played a pioneering role in promoting and safeguarding the new religious school of Srimanta Sankardev. The king not only provided him political refuge but also gave liberal grants to him. Much later Srimanta Sankardeva came to be regarded as one of the principal icons of Assamese cultural life. The Koch-Rajbangshis are also an integral part of Assam and Assamese nation. In much the same way the Bodos, the Karbis, the Dimasas, the Mishings have been an integral part of what is called the Assamese nation. Sadly with the rise in ethnic consciousness and narrowly conceived idea of modern post-colonial nationalism, the composite cultural identities are new breaking up into smaller identities. This book addresses some of these issues as to how ethnic identities are on the rise against the backdrop of Indian nationalism. The rise in print capitalism, vernacular languages and political ambition are also some of the issues which have played a great role in the rise of ethnic-nationalism. It will be interesting to research further on how print capitalism laid the inroads in Northeast India and created a conducive climate for the rise in ethnic nationalism.

2

The Assam Movement: Its Context and the Question of Nationalism

Ankita Baruah and Debabhuson Borah

Benedict Anderson's opinion that nations are 'imagined communities'[1] is perhaps relevant, albeit with some degree of reservations, to say that a discussion on nationalism is not beyond disagreement. Delving into the question of Assamese nationalism may be a hazardous occupation, on its own, as an unyielding Assamese nationalism does not seem to exist due to its assorted ethnic structure. An article even argues that the 'Assamese Nation' is an imagined one as is evident from the fact that there are distinct sub-nationalistic aspirations among disparate ethno-linguistic communities of Assam.[2] The tribes and communities living in Assam have their distinct cultural practices apart from what the term 'Assamese' inclusively covers. But the six-year-long Assam movement of 1979-85, the famous student agitation which continued for almost seven years, is widely considered as a manifestation of Assamese nationalistic sentiment. It opens up a number of imperative questions which need to be addressed while one discusses the Assam movement. Was the Assam movement simply a 'nationalistic' movement? Did it unite the Assamese society? An attempt will be made to examine the context and genesis of the Assam movement keeping these questions in mind.

Udayon Misra says that the answer to the question as to 'who is an Assamese?' opens up so many possibilities today that it has become necessary to do a historical analysis of the contentious issue of Assamese identity.[3] An array of contradictory views on Assamese nation has made it more complicated. This vital question has been addressed by many yet without unanimous consensus. While some merge it with religion and culture, some other sees there an expansion of caste. Although nationalism is regarded as both an ideology and a form of behavior, one thing, however, is apparent here that the growth of Assamese nationalism has been attached to the issues of Assamese language. There is no denying that tracing the historical context of Assamese nationalism is a problematic affair, but the orientation of language has been a central concern in the discourse of Assamese nationalism. Ambikagiri Raichoudhury (1885-1967), for instance, expressed that anyone who would embrace Assamese as his own language (mother tongue) was an Assamese.[4] He further opined that any community or ethnic group including the migrants which permanently resided in Assam and were ready to sacrifice for it, were all Assamese.[5]

There are some historical reasons for the rise of linguistic nationalism as a major element of Assamese nationalism. The historical and cultural disputes between the Assamese and Bengali language speakers are well-known. The British introduced Bengali language in schools and offices of Assam in 1837. As the Assamese middle class had awe for the Bengali language, they then did not oppose that step. Anandaram Dhekial Phukan (1829-59) and a few missionaries had raised voice in support of the Assamese language after some years and Assamese was reintroduced in schools and offices of Assam in 1873.

After independence, effort has been made by the Assamese middle class to make Assamese mandatory in all parts of the undivided Assam. The language movement (*bhasa andolon*) started in 1960 which opposed the Assam Official Language Bill. This movement created violence in many parts, particularly in Cachar where the Bengali-speaking people came in direct confrontation with the Assamese. The communal clashes led to the intervention of the Government of India. In 1972, there was another movement on the question of language. Like 1960, there were political and social violence between the Assamese and Bengali speakers. This led to the death of numbers of people.

Sangeeta Barooah Pisharoty's observation, in this context, is remarkable:

> Finally, talking of the cleaves that developed between the two communities in post-independent India would be incomplete if one does not take into account the fight for hegemony of language in Assam. Banking on the post-independent map of the state, Assam's third chief minister Bimala Prasad Chaliha made the first move to assert the linguistic jurisdiction of Assamese language over the entire state, including the Bengali-speaking people of Barak Valley, by bringing in an Official Language Bill in June 1960. It was the time when states were being recognized on the basis of language. The old tension between the two communities over language led to a reversal of roles and a vociferous resistance surfaced in Barak against the Bill.[6]

This conflict, nevertheless, had its root in migration, one of Assam's burning problems. On the other hand, the growing sense of Assamese nationalism, in a way, was a reciprocal phenomenon which developed simultaneously with the process of migration into Assam. It is needless to mention that Assam's migration problem had relatively a long history. The first major wave of state-sponsored migration to Assam began since the mid-19th century when the workers to the Assam's tea plantations were brought in from different parts of India. They were followed by migration of peasants from the districts of East Bengal to Assam. The British administrators in Assam wanted the fertile lands of the Brahmaputra valley to be opened up for jute cultivation by the peasants of East Bengal and jute produced in Assam would be supplied to Bengal jute industries.[7] Between 1900 and 1930s, several millions from the neighboring East Bengal (now Bangladesh) have settled down in the fertile lands of Assam to cultivate jute.[8] Assam also received large numbers of people from Nepal and according to 1971 census, Assam's Nepali population is 3.54 lakhs. Assam received a large group of Bengali petty traders, officials and workers belonging to Bengali, Marwari, and Bihari communities. By 1931 Indian Census, the Brahmaputra Valley received more than 5,76,000

East Bengali peasants and this number constituted 12.5 percent of Assam's total population.*

This massive migration really changed Assam's demographic character as well as the socio-political composition. Also, this had major impacts on Assam's political fate. Between 1937 and 1947 out of seven ministries formed in Assam, five were under the control of the Muslim League and the rest two by the Indian National Congress. Assam's Muslim League's Prime Minister (as the Chief Minister was known then) had also encouraged settlement of Muslim peasants during 1943 as part of the Grow More Food Campaign. This led to turbulent political debates in Assam before 1947. Assam's demography underwent massive change and it so happened that the British Cabinet Mission in 1946 grouped Assam with Bengal as part of its grouping proposal. The proposal of Assam's grouping with Bengal was opposed in Assam. The Muslim League under Muhammad Ali Jinnah (1876-1948) attempted to make Assam part of Pakistan supporting the proposal of Cabinet Mission. The leaders of Assam including Gopinath Bordoloi (1890-1950), the first CM of Assam in independent India, saved Assam from losing its identity with the help of Mahatma Gandhi (1869-1948).[9]

The migration to Assam did not stop even after independence. The influx from the East Pakistan to Assam continued despite consistent protest by its people. The Central Government was either reluctant or inactive to address this blazing concern of the people of Assam. Independence and *The Immigrants (Expulsion from Assam) Act, 1950* could hardly stop migration to Assam. As a result of continuous pressure from the Assam Government, however, the Foreigner's Tribunals were established in Assam

* According to 2011 Census, Assam's per square kilometer population density is 397 as against the all-India average of 382. Historically, till 1961 Assam's average density of population was lower than the all India average. [In 1901, Assam had 42 while the all-India average was 77 and in 1961 Assam's figure was 138 and the all India figure was 142.] Some major states of India have lower population density than that of Assam, i.e. Gujarat (308), Odisha (269), Telangana (307), Madhya Pradesh (236), Rajasthan (201) in 2011. Two states of NE India, Arunachal and Tripura's per kilometer population densities are 17 and 350 respectively.

in 1964 to detect and deport Pakistani migrants in Assam. The government also put in place a mechanism known as 'Prevention of Infiltration from Pakistan' to check illegal migration.

Assam had to face yet another phase of misfortune in 1971 while a treaty between Indira Gandhi (1917-84) and Mujibur Rahman (1920-75) was signed which set the deadline for the Hindus in East Pakistan to return to India as midnight 24 March 1971. So Assam received massive exodus of Hindus and Muslims from East Pakistan and many of them got their names enrolled in the revised electoral rolls in 1971. Basanta Deka writes:

> The Hindus and the Muslims, commonality being their Bengali language, who left during the struggle of Bangladesh and entered Assam, were quickly helped by the political parties to enroll their names in the electoral rolls. Just in one year, during 1970-71, the number of electors increased by ten percent![10]

The magnitude of illegal migration into Assam from 1901 to 1971 was indicated by the Registrar General of 1971:

> Taking the whole population of 3.29 million of Assam in 1901 as 'indigenous' and apply the all-India rate of increase of 129.67 from 1901 to 1971, its population in 1971 should have been 7.56 million instead of 14.63 million.[11]

Despite such havoc, the Government of India circular of 17 February 1976 nullified Jawaharlal Nehru's (1889-1964) proposal to treat 1952 as the 'date of enquiry' to determine citizenship of illegal immigrants as the circular stated that persons who had come to India from East Pakistan or Bangladesh prior to 24 March 1971 were not to be sent back to Bangladesh. This circular frustrated the indigenous people of Assam. The twin threat from the conspiracy to grow more Muslims and protect the Hindus was agitating the Assamese mind.

The issue of migration has been a major concern for the indigenous people of Assam since the British rule. This migration forced a large number of tribal people to get alienated from their lands. Tribal people and their leaders repeatedly warned the British Government before independence against the never-ending migration. The Report of the Census of India for the province of Assam for 1911 for the first time warned about the unabated migration to the province.** Distribution of lands to migrants also caused great alarm in Assam. For instance, in 1915 the Assam's colonial government passed a Land Settlement Policy. This policy made provisions for the distribution of lands to migrants. This government policy caused great outrage in Assam. *Times of Assam*, the leading newspaper from Assam on November 17, 1915 openly termed such policy as dangerous to Assam. On another occasion, on 13 March 1915, Manik Chandra Barua (1851-1915), member of the Assam Legislative Assembly Council, and first Indian Chairman of the Guwahati Municipality Board, demanded on the floor of the Assam Legislative Council that adequate measures be adopted to avoid conflicts between the local and migrant settlers. The Assam Association, Assam's solitary voice of the middle class, also publicly decried this land settlement policy of the government. A public meeting held on 17 March 1920 under the chairmanship of Tarun Ram Phukan (1877-1939) appealed the government to distribute land only to the people of Assam, not to migrants. In fact, the primary dispute and opposition between the Muslim League and Congress was centered on the question of land distribution with the migrant population. Migration from East Bengal and reclamation of land by the East Bengali migrants had greatly worried Assam's political leaders. Tribal and Assamese leaders have repeatedly drawn the attention of the government to regulate and stop this migration. By this time the number of tribal people losing their lands to the migrants had increased exponentially. In 1946, Gopinath Bordoloi resolved to evict the

** According to 2011 Census, Assam's per square kilometer population density is 397 as against the all-India average of 382. Historically, till 1961 Assam's average density of population was lower than the all India average. [In 1901, Assam had 42 while the all-India average was 77 and in 1961 Assam's figure was 138 and the all India figure was 142.] Some major states of India have lower population density than that of Assam, i.e. Gujarat (308), Odisha (269), Telangana (307), Madhya Pradesh (236), Rajasthan (201) in 2011. Two states of NE India, Arunachal and Tripura's per kilometer population densities are 17 and 350 respectively.

migrants who were settled in Assam's government lands and who came after 1 January 1938. After India's independence, the migration problem further intensified.[12]

Ambikagiri Raichoudhury and Gopinath Bordoloi pointed out how migration would in the long run hamper the political and cultural identity of Assam. Ambikagiri Raichoudhury and Nilmani Phukan (1880-1978) formed a unit within National Congress called 'Asomiya Sanrakhini Sabha' which submitted memorandum to Jawaharlal Nehru regarding the issue of migration into Assam and how it posed an economic crisis for its people. Gopinath Bordoloi strongly opposed the fact that Assam had to accommodate refuges despite her inability to do so. Leaders from across India supported the concerns articulated by the leaders of Assam. This led to the Indian Parliament to pass *The Immigrants (Expulsion from Assam) Act, 1950* which specifically ensured that Assam should not get any more refugees. But despite this, Assam received 2,73,000 Hindu refugees from East Pakistan according to the 1951 Census. By 1961 Census, this number has increased to 6,28,000.

So the issue of migration was the basic context of the Assam movement. It emerged as a protest to the migration into Assam. The negligence of the Central Government towards Assam also intensified its momentum. A kind of nationalistic sentiment centering on the 'Assamese' was thus instrumental due to such two-folded orientation. Nani Gopal Mahanta rightly holds that the twin concerns of the Assam movement were detection and deportation of illegal immigrants and step-motherly attitude of the Centre towards this peripheral state.[13]

The matter of illegal migration awfully disturbed the indigenous people of Assam. The immediate cause which boosted the Assam movement had a clear connection with it. The death of Hiralal Patwari, a member of Mangaldoi Lok Sabha constituency, demanded by-election. But immense increase of electorate was found in the electoral rolls. Simultaneously, a statement made on October 24, 1978 by S.L. Shakdher (1918-2002), then Chief Election Commissioner of India, that the unfathomable rise in the electorate in Assam was due to the influx of foreigners worsened the situation. Several organizations filed complaints demanding revised electoral rolls.

Finally, All Assam Students Union (AASU) called for Assam *bandh* on 8 June 1979 and all activities in Assam came to a halt. This was the beginning of the long movement. The initial objective of the movement was to throw out 'outsider' from Assam. The statement given by Bhrigu Kumar Phukan, the then General Secretary of AASU on June 3, 1979 clarifies the fact.[14] The term 'outsider' (*bohiragat*) initiated a controversy as it meant all people migrated to Assam even from other states of India. The AASU leadership tactfully changed the word from 'outsider' to 'foreigner' (*bideshi*) in the statement of 21 December 1979.[15] Whatever might be terminology and aim, there was little doubt that AASU began the movement seeking impartiality for the people of Assam. The AASU leaders demanded that the foreigners must leave Assam, their names from the electoral rolls must be removed and the border must be secured. The 'foreigners' were precisely the non-Assamese speakers who migrated into Assam from the East Pakistan. In the last part of August 1979, AASU formed the All Assam Gana Sangram Parishad, AAGSP, comprising of several organizations.

Thus, millions of people were in the street with the slogan *tej dim tel nidiu* (will give blood not oil) seeking a permanent solution to Assam's long migration problem. Various sections of the population engaged themselves in the movement to drive out the illegal migrants. 855 activists sacrificed their lives during the struggle. Several infamous incidents of violence such as Nellie massacre took place. A mob killed nearly 3000 people at Nellie on February 18, 1983 who belonged to the Muslim community of East Bengal origin.[16] This propelled a number of mob attacks in the region. The attack on the Bengali-Muslims in Chaulkhowa Chapori and the attack on the Assamese at Gohpur by the Bodo tribal group of Plain Tribal Council of Assam (PTCA) can be cited in this context. Assam thus witnessed mob violence, communities pitting against each other and breaking of community faithfulness during the last years of the movement. This indicates the violent nature of the movement which caused communal conflicts and brought a division among the people.

The agitation, however, finally forced the Government of India and Indian political leaders to recognize the problem of migrations to Assam. Under the Assam Accord, the Government of India undertook that all illegal immigrants who have come to Assam on or after 25 March 1971 would be detected and deported to the place of their country of origin. Also, all such deportation is to be carried out in accordance with the procedure laid down by the Government of India under the Foreigners Act, 1946 and the rules made thereafter. The Assam Accord, 1985 is a major political milestone in the political history of India's migration question, a landmark political solution to one of India's complex and deeply fraught problems. The Accord was signed on 14 August 1985 between the Indian Government and the leaders of Assam.

Certain socio-political changes in Assam during and after the movement raise several serious questions regarding the nationalistic sentiment that seemed instrumental behind the Assam movement. The Bodos, for instance, who could by no means call themselves other than Assamese have not only disdained to be known so, but even considered the word 'Assamese', a *bête noire*, a bugbear to be alarmed of.[17] What forced them to alienate themselves from all that is Assamese and agitate for complete identity for their own? It is important to note that certain sub-nationalistic aspirations grew in Assam among the tribal communities even during the British rule. The Bodos placed a memorandum in front of the Simon Commission in 1927 demanding special opportunities to them. The tribal people and the leaders of the tribal league became skeptical towards the Government of Assam due to the negligence towards them. Bhimbar Deuri (1903-47) in a debate in Assam legislative assembly in 1940, said:

> Most unfortunately to us and eternal shame to the section of people in whose hand, directly or indirectly, the Government of Assam had fallen for the last hundred years, the case of the tribal people, particularly of the plains, had been utterly neglected.[18]

Some scholars condemn the Assamese caste Hindus for perpetuating and aggravating the ethnic agitation in Assam.[19]

In an essay entitled "The Ethnic Agitation in Assam: Exploring the Roots", the author holds that the continual humiliation suffered by the ethnic groups in the hands of the caste Hindus caused an aversion amongst them to the so-called 'mainstream of Assamese life' whose dominant members were caste Hindus.[20] The author further criticized the role of the Assamese middle class for fueling such ethnic agitation. He considers the decision to impose the Assamese language as the only medium in schools and colleges as chauvinist activity as the decision was not made in consultations with the tribal organizations.[21]

It seems that the Assam Accord could not bring hope for several communities and sections in Assam. The Bodoland movement started in late 1980s demanding a separate state for the Bodos. Upendranath Brahma (1956-90) and his followers talked about discrimination against the Bodo people and initiated the Bodo movement just after the Assam Accord for a separate Bodoland which in turn took a very complex nature due to a section's involvement with armed struggle. Initially, All Bodo Students Union (ABSU) and other Plains Tribal organizations extended full support to the Assam movement. But in later years it became apparent that the real intention of the leaders of the movement was to establish Assamese regional hegemony, the tribal organizations, particularly the ABSU, started dissociating themselves from the movement.[22] The Bodos found no specific provision to safeguard their interests in the Assam Accord.[23] Likewise, the Mising community started demanding to establish Mising as the medium of instructions in all schools in the Mising-dominated regions. The leaders of the Dimasa community of North Cachar Hills demanded a separate state for the community. On the other hand, the Assam movement provided the platform for the growth of a secessionist force like United Liberation Front of Assam, which demands an independent Assam through fortified fight.[24] While some term the Assam movement as fascist and ultra-nationalistic,[25] its failure for not being able to be an inclusive movement of all the communities in Assam for fulfilling their aspirations is equally important. The minority groups in Assam also expressed their apprehensions time to time during and after the Assam movement. The students belonging to the minority communities organized themselves with political agenda by the union called All Assam Minority Students' Union (AAMSU) during the movement. After the Assam movement two political parties were formed concurrently; Assam Gana Parishad (AGP) and United Minorities Front (UMF). While the AGP was formed by the leaders of the Assam movement, the latter claimed to represent the religious and linguistic minorities of the state. Amalendu Guha (1924-2015) in his essay "Little Nationalism Turned Chauvinist: Assam's Anti-Foreigner Upsurge, 1979-80" says that Assam agitation was an attempt of the Assamese bourgeoisie to secure their political and cultural edge in Assam.[26] Guha considers this movement as a movement of the Assamese middle class terming it as 'little nationalism'.[27] All these throw considerable questions at a 'solid' Assamese nationalism and its upshot on the Assam movement.

Our study shows that the context of the Assam movement was predominantly influenced by the frequent waves of migration into Assam. Defining an Assamese has been a challenging occupation which pigeonholes Assamese nationalism as a special category. No doubt, the Assam movement was a mass movement and there was a nationalistic sentiment behind the movement. But the movement gradually lost the mass support after it turned violent during the Nellie massacre. Also, there was no integrated and universal Assamese nationalism as such which drove the Assam movement as it did not represent the sentiments of different tribes and communities living in Assam. In fact, some of them no longer wished to identify themselves as 'Assamese'. The movement could not unite the Assamese society as in one piece; rather, to an extent, some of its consequences contributed to damaging Assam's social fabric. The Assam movement, nevertheless, was a very crucial episode in the history of Assam. All these necessitate further exploration of the movement from other perspectives; as Assam's migration problem has not come to an end yet after more than 30 years of the Assam Accord.

Notes

1. Anderson, B. *Imagined Communities: Reflections on the Origin and Spread of Nationalism.* London: Verso, 1983
2. Paul, S. "Imagined Assamese Nationalism: Discourse on Identity Assertion and Sub-Nationalism in Assam" in https//ww.researchgate.net/publication/332263624
3. Misra, U. *India's North East.* New Delhi: OUP, 2014, p. 163.
4. Majumdar, P. "Asomt Jatiyatabadar Uthan Aru Sankatar Patabhumi" in *Asom Andolan: Pratisruti aru Phalasruti.* Guwahati: Banalata, 2001, p. 122.
5. *Ibid.*, p. 123.
6. Barooah Pisharoty, S. *Assam: The Accord, the Discord.* Gurgaon: Ebury Press, 2019, p. 261.
7. Kalita, R. "Prabajankarir Samasya aru Asom" in *Asom Andolan: Pratisruti aru Phalasruti.* Guwahati: Banalata, 2001, p. 12.
8. *Ibid.*, p. 13.
9. Deka, B. *The Design, the Betrayal, the Assam Movement.* Guwahati: Orchid Publication, 2015, p. 36.
10. *Ibid.*, p. 68.
11. *Ibid.*, p. 69.
12. Barooah Pisharoty, S. *Assam: The Accord, the Discord.* Gurgaon: Ebury Press, 2019, pp. 256-58.
13. Mahanta, N. *Confronting the State.* New Delhi: Sage, 2013, p. 31.
14. Nath, M. *Axom Andolon.* Guwahati: Aank-Baak, 2015, p. 105.
15. *Ibid.*, 106.
16. Barooah Pisharoty, S. *Assam: The Accord, the Discord.* Gurgaon: Ebury Press, 2019, p. 96.
17. Barman, S. "The Ethnic Agitation in Assam: Exploring the Roots" in *Ethnicity in Assam.* Dibrugarh: Centre for North-East Studies, 2001, p. 55.
18. Majumdar, P. "Asomt Jatiyatabadar Uthan Aru Sankatar Patabhumi" in *Asom Andolan: Pratisruti aru Phalasruti.* Guwahati: Banalata, 2001, p. 132.
19. Barman, S. "The Ethnic Agitation in Assam: Exploring the Roots" in *Ethnicity in Assam.* Dibrugarh: Centre for North-East Studies, 2001, p. 58.
20. *Ibid.*, p. 61.
21. *Ibid.*, p. 62.
22. ABSU document *Why Separate State?*, 1987, pp. 310-15.

23. *Ibid.*, p. 312.
24. Mahanta, N. *Confronting the State*. New Delhi: Sage, 2013, p. 33.
25. Jana, Jyotirmoy. "Andolan aru Motantar" in *Asom Andolan: Pratisruti aru Phalasruti*. Guwahati: Banalata, 2001, p. 154.
26. Guha, A. "Little Nationalism Turned Chauvinist: Assam's Anti-Foreigner Upsurge, 1979-80" in *Economic and Political Weekly*, Vol. 15, No. 41/43, p. 1702.
27. *Ibid.*, p. 1703.

References

Anderson, B. *Imagined Communities: Reflections on the Origin and Spread of Nationalism*. London: Verso, 1983.

Barooah Pisharoty, S. *Assam: The Accord, the Discord*. Gurgaon: Ebury Press, 2019.

Baruah, S. Ed. *Beyond Counter-Insurgency: Breaking the Impasse in North East India*. New Delhi: OUP, 2009.

——. *India Against Itself: Assam and the Politics of Nationality*. New Delhi: OUP, 1999.

Brass, Paul R. *Ethnicity and Nationalism: Theory and Comparison*. New Delhi: Sage, 1999.

Cohen, J.L. "Strategy or Identity: New Theoretical Paradigms and Contemporary Social Movement" in *Social Research*, Vol. 52, No. 4, Winter 1985.

Deka, B. *The Design, the Betrayal, the Assam Movement*. Guwahati: Orchid Publication, 2015.

Deka, K.M. and Phukan, K.N. Ed. *Ethnicity in Assam*. Dibrugarh: Centre for North-East Studies, 2001.

Gohain, H. and Borah, D. Ed. *Asom Andolan: Pratisruti aru Phalasruti*. Guwahati: Banalata, 2001.

Hussain, M. *Assam Movement: Class, Ideology and Identity*. New Delhi: Manak Publications, 1993.

Mahanta, N. *Confronting the State*. New Delhi: Sage, 2013.

Misra, U. *India's North East*. New Delhi: OUP, 2014.

——. *The Periphery Strikes Back*. Shimla: IIAS, 2000.

Nath, M. *Axom Andolan*. Guwahati: Aank-Baak, 2015.

3

Nationalism and Minority Politics in Assam: A Look at AIUDF's Performance

Parvin Sultana

Political parties are important institutions of a democracy. Multicultural democratic societies have witnessed the growth of political parties which represent the interest of different groups. Many parties claim to represent the interests of specific groups, ethnic communities etc. Ethnic political parties now flourish across the democratic world. Canada, Spain, India, the United Kingdom, Israel, Sri Lanka, Macedonia, South Africa and Russia are only a few examples of the established or emerging democracies in which they have taken root (Chandra, 2004). An ethnic party is a party which claims to overtly represent the interests of the cause of one particular ethnic category or set of categories to the exclusion of others, and that makes such a representation central to its strategy of mobilizing voters.

Chandra defines a multiethnic party as one which makes appeal related to ethnicity central to its mobilizing strategy but that assumes a position of neutrality or equidistance toward all other relevant categories. Parties which don't appeal to voters on ethnic lines can be termed as non-ethnic parties. Parties can be categorized as such based on its support base and the message it send across to prospective voters in the form of manifesto, representation, co-option of leaders from newer ethnic communities, etc.

Political parties emerge in a concrete social and political milieu. Yogendra Yadav mentions two such crucial moments in India's political life which witnessed the emergence of newer political parties. He called them democratic upsurges. The first was in late 1960s which saw the decline of the 'Congress system' in which Congress dominated (the period of 1952-67), and began an era where Congress retained the position of 'natural party of governance' but anti-Congressism allowed opposition parties to challenge it in states.

The second upsurge was during 1990s that saw a higher voter turn-out, greater political mobilization of marginalised communities and availability of new political choices before the voters (Yadav, 2000). This witnessed the emergence of a large number of regional and ethnic parties in India. The 1990s witnessed the emergence of the BJP as well as the shift to state as the space where party politics unfolded. Since there was an end of Single Party Majority (SPM) governments and an era of coalition was ushered in, no Central Government could be formed without the support of state parties. Barring a few states like Rajasthan, Gujarat, Madhya Pradesh, all the states have their political space divided between the all-India parties and some State-level party or parties. These State-level parties represent a wide range of social forces and ideological opinions (Palshikar, 2003).

While there is a certain amount of fuzziness, some broad 'ideological zones' emerged amongst the political parties. One ideological zone is represented by the rhetoric of social justice (Rashtriya Janata Dal, Samajwadi Party, BSP, etc.). Another is represented by regional identity (National Conference, Akali Dal, AGP, DMK, AIADMK, etc.). The third ideological zone would be characterised by the developmental logic (TDP, BJD). The fourth ideological zone is occupied by the idea of political Hindutva. The fifth is the ideology of neo-liberalism (Congress, BJP and many others). The sixth zone is represented by the anti-globalisation position (Palshikar, 2004).

Ethnic Parties in Democracy

Ethnic divisions and its manifestation in the emergence of newer ethnic parties are at times seen as a threat to democracy.

While according to one side of the debate exemplified by the works of Alvin Rabushka and Kenneth Shepsle, the threat is insurmountable. According to the other side, exemplified by Robert Dahl, it can sometimes be mitigated. But they all agree that ethnic diversity is inversely related to the maintenance of democracy. Chandra on the other hand states that ethnic parties sustain democracy, depending on the institutional context within which ethnic divisions are politicized (Chandra, 2005). Chandra while studying the ethnic parties in India especially Bahujan Samaj Party argues that instead of depoliticizing the issues that ethnic group are most likely to fight over, or constrain the power of ethnic majorities to make unilateral decisions on issues that concern ethnic minorities, she suggests that institutions for multiethnic democracies should encourage the politicisation of ethnic divisions and induce proliferation of multiple ethnic majorities. In Chandra's opinion, a multitude of freely forming ethnic majorities may be a more effective safeguard against the destabilization of democracy than the imposition of constraints on any single one. In India, such ethnic mobilisation is undertaken through policies like affirmative action, language policy, recognition of statehood, etc. While Chandra believes that rise of ethnic parties do not concede a threat to democratic stability, many scholars are of the view that the second democratic upsurge did not deepen Indian democracy in true sense. Many political theorists were unsure of the rise of the plebeian politics. Another challenge to the idea that post 1990s, India's democracy became more participatory comes from scholars who believe Indian democracy is a sham. This view is found in the writings of Jalal (1995), Brass (1990), Vanaik (1990), etc. According to these scholars, changes at the level of elections and elected institutions are of little consequence so long as the social and economic inequalities of civil society remain unaltered. For these scholars, elections in India are just a "ritual" and the rise of ethnic parties does not necessarily translate to the development of these very communities. Ashutosh Varshney points out that while these limitations need to be taken on board, the deepening of India's democracy can at best be called an unfinished development. These scholars point out the limitations of procedural democracy and reiterates that procedural democracy often constraints substantive democracy.

While many battles for social dignity and equality for the lower castes still lie ahead, India's democracy has in fact paved a way for such struggles. In India, unlike many other democracies, the incidence of voting is higher among the poor than among the rich, among the less educated than among the graduates, in the villages than in the cities (Yadav, 1996). While there is a need to move beyond procedural democracy towards substantive democracy, it is important to acknowledge political rights that a democracy bestows (Varshney, 2000). Along with the changing nature of party system in India, coalition government prompted the rise of regional parties. While many were alarmed that newer regional parties will lead to further fragmentation of democracy, the regional parties of this day are different. While newer parties may have a narrow regional support base, they are not regionalist, i.e. most parties of today do not invoke regionalism. In a coalition era, regional parties are not pitted against national parties, rather they are partners and hence cannot be antagonistic to interests of national parties (Ziegfeld, 2012).

Muslim Politics and Political Parties in Assam: The Colonial Period

Political parties have been crucial agents of politics and Assam was no stranger to rise of newer political parties which provided strong alternatives to national political parties. From the rise of strong regionalist party like the Asom Gana Parishad to the multi-ethnic party All India United Democratic Front (AIUDF), Assam's political party system have undergone much change. To understand the rise of new parties like AIUDF, it is important to revisit colonial history. Until 1937, Muslims did not play a significant role in the region's politics and it was the Indian National Congress that was gradually emerging as the dominant force. The Muslim community was a fragmented one and it was reflected in their politics. The Assamese Muslims did not always side with the migrant Muslim population. It was as late as in 1944 that the divergent trends merged.

In Assam, the Assam Pradesh Muslim League was formed in the district of Sylhet in late 1920s by Abdul Matin Chowdhury. In the first election to the Assam Legislative Assembly under the Government of India Act, 1935, four League members were elected for the first time. In the Brahmaputra Valley, a branch was established by Maulana Abdul Hamid Khan Bhashani. Since the inauguration of provincial autonomy under the Government of India Act, 1935, political development in Assam led to the emergence of a distinct migrant Muslim lobby which in course of time, became a powerful force under the leadership of Maulana Bhashani. While Bhashani tried to organize the working class and oppressed peasants of Bengal and Assam, he soon fell out with the Muslim League, too, after Sir Saadullah formed the Muslim League Government in Assam as he felt that the government went against the interest of migrant Muslim peasants. As opposed to the demands of Maulana Bhashani, Sir Saadullah was not keen on abolishing the Line System altogether. Sworn in on 1 April 1937 Sir Saadullah's ministry was a short lived one. Opposed by Muslim League, he had to lean on the European bloc. He soon realised that he will need the support of his co-religionists from the Surma valley who formed the majority of Assembly's Muslim members (Guha, 226). Saadullah and his supporters joined the Muslim League. He formed a new ministry with Abdul Matin Chowdhury, Munawwar Khan, etc. The most crucial issue for Sir Saadullah's ministry was the question of Line System and how to regulate migration. In early 1938, he tried to mitigate the crisis by appointing an enquiry committee to look into the working of the Line System.

After this Saadullah's ministry was replaced by a Congress coalition headed by Gopinath Bordoloi. But as this ministry had to resign soon at the advent of the Second World War, it could not spell out a clear policy on migration. When Saadullah formed the ministry again, the biggest challenge continued to be the question of the Line system. Saadullah found himself caught between the abolitionists and segregationists. In May 1940, the Saadullah Ministry called a conference in Shillong to discuss the desirable changes with regard to migrants and Line System. However, in this conference, the question of abolition was kept aside and some kind of protective mechanism for the indigenous tribal population was to be sorted. Earmarking the date of 1 January 1938, those who came before it were to be systematically settled. However, Sir Saadullah's initiatives didn't satisfy the leaders of migrant Muslim community. Matiur Rahman Miya of Goalpara complained that in 1940, at the Assam Provincial Muslim League Conference, the premier promised to give land to the landless but failed to do so (Guha, 258). Bhashani was also very critical of Sir Saadullah for failing to abolish Line System. Amidst such pressure, Sir Saadullah's government took up the 'Grow More Food Programme' to dilute the restrictions imposed by the Line System. This programme aimed at resuming redistribution of wastelands in accordance to need of various communities and de-reserve certain grazing reserves in Nagaon, Kamrup, and Darrang. This programme provided a grand opportunity to keep the Line System at abeyance and make settlements of land with the migrants at an unprecedented pace. The government in fact decided to accelerate land settlement in Kamrup, Nowgong, and Darrang to extend areas of migrant colonies and to settle more lands with migrants owing to the imperative need of growing more food.

Muslim politics in the colonial period in Assam revolved around the question of migration. While initially it was encouraged, very soon the changed demography of the state led to the leaders of the indigenous people demand for protection. M. Kar's work points out how in the first decade of 20th century middle class Assamese encouraged migration which provided cheap labour. But with changing demography, the attitude towards fresh waves of migration changed. The pre-independence period is marred by compulsion to draw a line between migrants who came earlier and hence should be given the rights to settle and fresh migrants.

Muslim Politics and Political Parties in Post-Colonial Assam

With partition, the Muslims who stayed back in India did not continue their support of the Muslim League. The fresh inflow of Hindu migrants again raised the fears of indigenous Assamese people. Pitted again against Bengalis, they found allies in the migrant Muslims who came to be regarded as Na-Assamiya and who accepted Assamese language and culture. In the words of Myron Weiner:

> After 1947, the Bengali Muslims became the de facto allies of the Assamese in their conflict with the Bengali Hindus. Bengali Muslims have been willing to accept Assamese as the medium of instruction in their schools, and they have thrown their votes behind the Assamese candidates for the state assembly and the national Parliament. They have declared Assamese as their mother-tongue. In return the state government has not attempted to eject Bengali Muslims from lands on which they have settled in the Brahmaputra valley, though earlier leaders had claimed that much of the settlement had taken illegally...there is an unspoken coalition between the Assamese and the Bengali Muslims against the Bengali Hindus. (Weiner, 1978; 124)

However, this coalition did not smoothen out all problems. The continued migration to the state further accelerated by the Freedom Movement of Bangladesh rekindled the issue of the threat of unabated migration. Opposing such migration, a state wide movement grew. The Assam Movement lasted for six long years from 1979 to 1985. However, newer trends in Muslim politics in Assam started emerging even before that. The discontent of Muslims with their new ally, the Congress was visible as early as 1975, when in the month of February, a Guwahati Convention was held under the inspiration of Parliamentary Affairs Minister, Syed Ali Ahmed and supported by Moinul Haque Choudhury. Ali presided over the Open Session and the convention discussed the problems faced by 40 lakh Muslims in Assam. Speakers from both the valley talked about 'obstacles' that constrained Muslim participation in all spheres and branches of life (Kar, 1990: 359). The meeting ended with a decision to form a Muslim Parishad with Syed Ahmed Ali as the President for safeguarding and promoting Muslim interests. It was to be a non-political body and would also work in tandem with Muslims in other part of the country. Many however complained that it was an initiative of Muslim ministers to strengthen their own position. The organisation was finally dissolved by the President in 1975 without any cogent justification.[1]

After it the feasible alternative seemed like a separate political party for the Muslims. Following the Congress debacle in the Lok Sabha election in 1977, a section of educated Muslims gathered at Haji Musafir Khana, Islampur, Guwahati on May 9, 1977. The meeting was presided by Mr Amjad Ali, Advocate, Ex-Vice-President, Assam Provincial Muslim League and ex-MP and attended by delegates from all over Assam. The discussion quoted problems like disillusionment with Congress and its motives as well as the denial of equal rights and privileges to Muslims (Kar, 1990: 360).

In view of all this, it was decided that a new political party under the name of Eastern India Muslim Association (EIMA) with headquarters at Guwahati. The new party had the following objectives like working for the unity and integrity of the nation but at the same time protect and safeguard the rights of the Muslims. It further stated that it will work to propagate among Muslims ideas of nationalism, democracy, socialism and secularism, etc.[2] The Executive Committee of the party was headed by Abdul Muhib Mazumdar, Advocate, Gauhati High Court and had five Vice-Presidents, four secretaries and one treasurer. Representation was given to Assam, Manipur, Tripura, and Meghalaya. District offices were set up in Cachar, Darrang, Goalpara, Kamrup, and Nowgong. Fifty thousand members were enrolled till 1979 (Kar, 1990: 363).

On the eve of Assembly elections of 1978, selected Muslim leaders met at Gauhati and decided to form the Progressive Democratic Front which consisted of EIMA, Kamata Rajya Parishad, Janata Congress, Yuva Linguistic Minority Committee and Citizens Democratic Front. The candidates were put as independents. It captured five seats, one each in Darrang, Kamrup, Nowgong and two in Lakhimpur. EIMA won two seats in Kamrup and Lakhimpur.[3] The Eastern India Muslim Association was formally dissolved in October 1977 to re-emerge as the Eastern Zonal Muslim League. While it opposed unabated migration, it also questioned the harassment meted out on Indian Muslims in the name of finding out infiltrators. The Association also tried to co-operate with other regional organisations and did not work exclusively for Muslims.

After this, in the background of the signing of Assam Accord in 1985, another organisation named the United Minority Front, Assam was formed. This party was formed only 15 days prior to the elections. It tried to unite both Bengali Hindus and Bengali Muslims. A convention was held in the district of Nowgong under the leadership of A.F. Golam Osmani on 9 and 10 November 1985. Almost 3000 delegates participated from organisations like All Assam Minority Students Union, Citizens Right Preservation Committee, All Assam Minority Yuva Parishad and some other tribal organisations.

Initially, it received the support of the Hindus and the Muslims of East Bengal origin. It contested in the Assam Assembly Elections in 1985 and won 17 seats and one Lok Sabha seat. But it too could not survive because of internal contradictions (Ahmed, 2018: 32). Later it also allied with AGP against Congress. Electorally, it got very weakened and was no more an alternative for the Muslims.

After UMFA, it was in 2005 that another political party was formed which tried to address the problems that ails the minority community. Few incidents are regarded as the immediate cause of the formation of the party. In 2005 in Golaghat district's Negheribil area, a group of people from lower Assam were heckled by some local organisations as being allegedly Bangladeshis. These people who mostly work as daily wage earners, in brick kilns, as rickshaw pullers were threatened to leave their work and go back home. After this, the Illegal Migration Detection by Tribunal Act which was seen by many as a shield against harassment was scrapped by the Supreme Court on 10 March 2005.

In such a situation, the Jamiat Ulema i Hind organised a meeting on 25 May 2005 at the Haji Musafirkhana. Most minority organisations participated in the meeting and a co-ordination committee was formed. This co-ordination committee held meetings with different organisations of the state like the

All Assam Students Union (AASU), Jatiyotabadi Yuva Satro Parishad, Asom Sahitya Sabha, etc. While these meetings did mitigate the tension, there was a sense of insecurity prevailing amidst the community. The Congress's failure to uphold the IMDT Act also disillusioned a section of the community. To fill the void, the co-ordination committee organised a meeting on 2 October 2005 in which it was decided that a political platform will be created to voice the concerns of the marginalised groups. The then President of Jamiat, Maulana Badruddin Ajmal became the founder President of the newly formed United Democratic Front (UDF). Later it was named All India United Democratic Front (AIUDF).[4]

The Electoral Promises

The 2016 elections set a defining campaign. It showed newer social alignments put in place. The four major political parties Congress, BJP, AIUDF, and AGP tried to woo voters on different issues. The AGP has presence in most of the constituencies and enjoyed acceptance in the constituencies with a substantial number of Muslims. In terms of representation, AGP has tried to provide adequate representation to the Muslims. A reason for the lack lustre performance of UMFA is also the fact that many Muslims supported AGP. It is believed that Congress was voted out of power in 1996 and AGP was able to form the government because Muslims supported AGP. If we look at elections since 1985, we will notice that AGP gave tickets to a large number of Muslims. However with the coming of AIUDF, the hold of AGP over the Muslims slackened a bit. Earlier AGP has done well in constituencies with a substantial number of Muslim voters. In 1996, it won the Sonai Assembly seat. Abdul Aziz, the AGP candidate was elected from Rupahihat in 2006 and Khalilur Rahman Choudhury was elected twice from Jamunamukh in 1996 and 2001. While the party did ally with BJP for the 2016 elections, it did not aim at alienating the Muslims. Even for 2016 elections it emphasised on solving the problem of illegal immigration, implementation of Assam Accord, protection of Assamese language and culture, unemployment, etc. The party unlike its ally did not differentiate between immigrants on the basis of religion.

Coming to the next party, the AIUDF emphasised on issues like that of D voters, which affected many of East Bengal origin Muslims. While AIUDF also stated clearly in its manifesto that it opposes illegal immigration and makes no distinction among foreigners on the basis of religion, it did point out the anomalies that are prevalent in the procedure of finding out D voters. It has earlier also spoken against the procedural loopholes when a large number of women were detained for lack of proper documents.

The BJP's manifesto highlighted some of the pressing problems that the state has faced for a very long time. Starting from the illegal infiltration of foreign nationals to the implementation of the Accord, it tried to cover the major issues. Other crucial issues were insurgency, floods, land erosion, etc. While there is a popular belief that the BJP is an 'untouchable' party for the Muslims, since 2014 the perception might have changed. The party recognising that the community is electorally a deciding factor in a number of constituencies did try to reach out. And as a proof of this realisation, the vision document of BJP under the sub-heading 'Religious Minorities Welfare' have touched upon issues that influence the religious minorities. It talked of safeguarding the interests of indigenous Muslim communities like the Goria, Moria, and Deshi. It also talked of capacity building in char areas and skill development along with a greater emphasis on women education. The Congress while pointing out some of its achievements in the last three terms also took up pressing issues like the alleged harassment of Muslims in the name of finding D voters. It also talked about the infrastructural development of minority areas and linking these areas with markets, storage facilities, etc.

The Campaign

From the very beginning, the BJP succeeded in taking on board the parties that claimed to represent the indigenous communities. To start with, a pre-election alliance between the BJP and the Bodo People's Front (BPF) was the first alliance brokered by BJP in the early days of 2016. Subsequently, BJP also succeeded in taking the leaders of Rabha and Tiwa tribes along with them. A major gain of BJP was taking AGP on board. The regional political party which has been away from the corridors of power for long enough saw an opportunity in this alliance especially in the light of 2014 elections. This strategic alliance played a crucial part in ensuring a landslide victory of the BJP. While it cannot be overlooked that the field for BJP has been prepared by Sangh working in the ground level (Bhattacharjee, 2016), BJP succeeded in ensuring that this was underplayed by constantly harping on the popular slogan of Jati, Mati, and Bheti which roughly translates as nationality, land and the hearth (Misra, 2016). The campaign constantly tried to realign the communities around the discourse of 'Us' versus the 'Others'. BJP successfully portrayed itself as the saviour of the 'indigenous people' and could transform it to electoral gains. Udayon Misra (2016) argues that the BJP's landslide victory in Assam had to do with the success of BJP in garnering the support of regional forces like the Asom Gana Parishad, the Bodoland People's Front and the Rabha, Tiwa and other tribal organisations (Misra, 2016, p. 20). He further points out that the emphasis in the campaign was on preserving the identity and culture of the people of Assam and not to put forth a Hindutva ideology.

A Study of Dhubri

To understand how the Muslims voted in 2016 elections, this paper will look at the district of Dhubri and the Assembly election results of the seven constituencies. Dhubri is located in the westernmost part of Assam. It has a population of 1,948,632. It is one of the nine Muslim majority districts of Assam with a Muslim population comprising 74.29%. The results of the seven constituencies of Dhubri show how the Muslim electorate in the district voted. It is important as it also resonates with the voting pattern of the community at large.

South Salmara

South Salmara has the highest concentration of Muslims. Affected badly by flood and erosion, the constituency lags behind on most fronts. While the popular belief is that Muslims comprise a vote bank of the Congress, this Muslim majority constituency proved otherwise. It returned Dewan Joynal Abedin, an SUCI candidate, to the Assembly thrice in 1978, 1985, and 1991. With the emergence of AIUDF, the party made this constituency its stronghold and it won elections from this constituency in 2006 and 2011. However, in 2016, the result of the elections from Salmara Constituency was very interesting. Badruddin Ajmal, the sitting MP of Dhubri constituency himself contested from South Salmara earlier held by his son Abdur Rahman Ajmal. However, in 2016, Badruddin Ajmal lost to Congress candidate Wazed Ali Choudhury. Wazed Choudhury had earlier represented the constituency. People voted for Ajmal in 2006 because they expected development on crucial markers like health, education, etc. However, ten years down the line, the condition of the people in the ground level did not improve much. Many were disillusioned with the tactics of Ajmal like distributing holy water as a response to the problems of the people. As a result, he lost by a margin of 16723 votes.

Dhubri

While in South Salmara, Muslims did not vote for AIUDF, in the neighbouring constituencies of Dhubri and Gauripur, the AIUDF candidates Nazrul Hoque and Nizanur Rahman won with excellent margins. In Dhubri AIUDF candidate Nazrul Hoque got 60933 and won by a margin of 24086. Dhubri saw a close three-way competition between ex-Congress MLA and Minister Nazibul Umar who contested as an independent candidate, Dr. Debamoy Sanyal of BJP and Nazrul Hoque of AIUDF. With Congress candidate Abedur Zaman getting mere 13000 votes and Dr. Sanyal getting 33000 votes, it would seem that voters in this Muslim dominated constituency voted for AIUDF to keep BJP from winning the seat. Congress votes have shifted to both Nazibul Umar and AIUDF's Nazrul Hoque.

In Dhubri, AIUDF denied nomination to the sitting MLA Jahanuddin and gave ticket to Nazrul Hoque. Similarly, Congress denied veteran leader Nazibul Umar nomination and gave the ticket to Abedur Zaman. Jahanuddin openly supported Nazibul Umar when he decided to contest as an independent candidate. A conversation with voters in a Muslim majority pocket brought forth that Muslims who traditionally voted for Congress backed AIUDF to ensure that there is no massive vote split.

Gauripur

A similar picture is seen in Gauripur. Traditional Congress voters voted for AIUDF's Nijanur Rahman who got 73423 votes and won by a margin of 19911 votes. Voters felt that Congress candidate Sushil Kumar Roy will not be able to stop BPF's sitting MLA Banendra Mushahary from winning and hence they voted for the AIUDF candidate. Nijanur Rahman also contested in 2011 when he got 37190 votes. Factors like anti-incumbency played a big role in deciding how people cast their votes. Despite the change in the election results, it is to be remembered by Banendra Mushahary has won earlier and this time it seems votes shifted from Congress to AIUDF and led to the win of Nijanur Rahman.

Bilasipara East

Muslims have voted strategically and not as a vote bank. In many constituencies Muslims voted for BJP-AGP alliance. For example, in the Muslim dominated East Bilasipara constituency, BJP candidate Ashok Shinghi won and it could not have been possible without Muslim votes. East Bilasipara has a total population of 184994 and it saw a 90.41% voter turnout. BJP's Ashok Singhi won the election with total votes of 59206 and defeated the Congress candidate Amrit Badsha by a margin of 5096. The margin has however lessened since earlier elections pointing to shifts in votes. In the previous election in 2011 AIUDF candidate Gul Akhtara Begum defeated AGP's candidate Prashanta Kumar Barua by a margin of around 24,425 votes. While this year, the votes of the winner rose by around ten thousand, the vote-share of the runner up has also increased. But here one thing should be remembered that Bilasipara also elected AGP's Prashanta Barua on many occasions. So, the basis of voting has not always been on communal lines. Singhi as a businessman enjoyed a level of acceptance amongst the religious minorities. After the election results were declared, he categorically stated that he would work for the all-round development of the community. He is not perceived as someone with a communal agenda.

Bilasipara West

Bilasipara West saw AIUDF retain its seat and Hafiz Bashir Ahmed succeeded in defeating independent candidate Ali Akbar Miah with a margin of around ten thousand votes. Ali Akbar Miah has contested earlier from other parties like AGP, NCP, INC, etc. and this time when denied ticket he decided to contest as an independent. While he could retain a good electoral support, he could not defeat the sitting MLA. Hafiz Bashir Ahmed has been the MLA of Bilasipara West since its inception in 2006.

Golakganj

Golakganj is an interesting case as the sitting Congress MLA Abu Taher Bepari defected to BJP. However, he was denied ticket and Ashwini Kumar Ray was given nomination. The constituency has earlier sent CPI candidates Alauddin Sarkar to the Assembly, BJP candidate Dinesh Sarkar etc. So, the 2016 elections was not exactly a surprise and despite close competition, Ashwini Ray won by a margin of 6391. It was a gain for BJP as the constituency was held by INC for the last two terms.

Mankachar

Mankachar returned Dr. Motior Rahman Mondol who defeated Aminul Islam of AIUDF. The seat was earlier held by Zabed Islam who rebelled from Congress for being denied nomination. The political scenario is also decided by the faction within the family of ex Minister Zahirul Islam. The election results of Dhubri shows that the Muslims have voted in different ways. While in South Salmara it sent a crucial message to Ajmal by defeating him, in Dhubri and Gauripur the electorate backed AIUDF to ensure that BJP did not come to power. In Bilasipara East Muslims voted for BJP because they wanted an alternative and believed in the promise of development. Apart from this if we look at some other districts, we will also see that Muslims especially Assamese Muslims did vote for the BJP-AGP alliance.

A fraction of Bengali Muslims voted for the BJP in Barkhetri, Sipajhar and Sorbhog to defeat Congress. While in Barak valley, AIUDF performed better riding on the anti-Congress wave, in Sonai BJP's Aminul Haque Laskar made the most of the competition between AIUDF and Congress.

BJP fielded around 6 Muslim candidates in 2016. And it succeeded in making inroads in all parts of Assam. In Guwahati East, BJP candidate and former state President Siddhartha Bhattacharya won by a huge margin of 96,637 votes and it would not have happened without the support of the Muslims. Even in Barpeta, Morigaon and Nagaon BJP succeeded in getting Muslim votes. The election results in Sonai constituency also throw some interesting facts. While the BJP showed a remarkable increase in vote-share from 24.72% in 2014 to 35.83% in 2016, the Congress experienced a fall by 5.40% (Ahmed, 2018). In a multi cornered battle the BJP won but its vote-share was not very high. Interestingly the combined vote-share of AIUDF and Congress surpassed that of BJP, but the split of votes worked in favour of the BJP candidate. The AIUDF took away a large slice of Congress vote in 2016.

AIUDF: A Decline?

AIUDF's electoral performance has seen a downward curve since 2016. In 2018 Panchayat elections and 2019 Parliamentary elections, AIUDF fared poorly. The Panchayat elections of Assam took place amidst strong protests against the Citizenship Amendment Bill, 2016. While many contemplated that BJP will not do well, the results say otherwise. While BJP emerged victorious with the highest number of seats in every category, AIUDF has performed extremely badly.

In fact, AIUDF's stronghold Jamunamukh has been breached. BJP and Congress candidates have won in many Gaon Panchayats of Jamunamukh. The elections which were held on 5th and 9th of December saw a sharp decline in the support base of AIUDF. In Jamunamukh, Hojai and Lumding—Congress led followed by BJP, AIUDF and AGP.

The 2018, Panchayat elections saw AIUDF almost decimated. In the last Panchayat elections held in 2013, AIUDF had second position. But this time the party was relegated to almost fourth position. Let us take a look at the final tally of 2018:

Post	Total	BJP	Congress	AGP	AIUDF
GP Members	21970	9094	7292	1689	1024
GP President	2197	994	760	137	130
AP Members	2197	1025	771	118	139
ZP Members	420	212	147	19	26

Source: Assam State Election Commission website

It is clear that AIUDF performed very poorly. The gap between Congress which got the second position and AIUDF is very high. This points to a significant shift of votes of AIUDF to Congress. AIUDF's support base has been breached in places like Dhubri, Goalpara, Karimganj, Cachar, Barpeta, Darrang, Morigaon.

Let us also look at AIUDF's performance in 2013 vis-a-vis 2018

Post	2013	2018
GP Members	2623	1024
GP Presidents	387	130
AP Members	397	139
ZP Members	76	26

In Assam, the trend has always been that the ruling party always wins the local self-governments. Also the gap between the winning party and the party which secures second position is often very high. In 2013, Congress won 273 seats in the category of Zila Parishad members and the AIUDF which secured second position won only 76 seats. But if we look at the tally of 2018, while BJP succeeded in winning more than 50% seats in the Panchayat elections, the gap between BJP and the Congress is not very high. While BJP won 212 ZPC members, Congress is not very far at 147. In 2013 Panchayat elections, Congress had won 273 ZPC seats while the second ranking AIUDF could grab only 76 seats, with BJP winning only 15 seats. The AGP had won

29 seats but in 2018 could win only 19 seats.[5] BJP on its own captured the ZPC at Barak Valley. And has succeeded in bagging absolute majority in Tinsukia, Dibrugarh, Sonitpur, Kamrup, Kamrup metro, Biswanath, Lakhimpur, Nalbari, Golaghat, Charaideo, Dhemaji and Majuli. Congress along with Cachar ZPC, Congress won in Barpeta, Karimganj, Jorhat, Morigaon and Dhubri. AIUDF on its own could get only Hailakandi and South Salmara.

In 2013, AIUDF has won 76 ZPC seats and in 2018 it has declined by 65% and AIUDF has managed to win only 26 seats. Its vote-share also dropped by 13% in 2016 Assembly seats. It seems that the Bengali Muslims vote has shifted to Congress in 2016 to keep BJP out and even in Panchayat elections, this did not change. After almost 15 years, AIUDF does not seem to be a very strong alternative for Muslims. Many accuse AIUDF of acting as the B team of BJP and ensuring that they won in many places. There is an element of disillusionment with AIUDF and that was reflected in the Panchayat results as well. Few factors responsible for such an outcome are firstly, people prefer their local representative to be from the ruling party. This is crucial to ensure that developmental fund does not get affected. Secondly, Muslims seem to have largely gravitated to the Congress. While in 2013 and 2016, Muslims voted for AIUDF in large numbers, the anti-Muslim rhetoric of BJP pushed many Muslims towards Congress.[6] The tally shows that the biggest loser in the Panchayat elections has been AIUDF followed by AGP. Not only issues like NRC and Citizenship Amendment Bill has not affected BJP's performance, but BJP has also improved largely on its 2013 seat and vote-share. However, this may not be a landslide for BJP as Congress performed better even after being in power for 12 years and other parties were decimated. But in 2018, Congress is not lagging far behind and the gap between the two parties is not very high.

In 2019 elections, AIUDF took an interesting decision. It decided to fight at only three seats—Dhubri, Karimganj and Barpeta. While this was allegedly done to ensure that opposition votes don't get divided, this move was criticized by the BJP as an understanding between the Congress and the AIUDF. This move however did not bring much success to either parties—while Congress managed to win only three seats, AIUDF managed to retain only the seat of Badruddin Ajmal. In the by-elections however AIUDF could win one seat while BJP managed to win two seats.

Conclusion

2016 can be regarded as a watershed moment in Assam's politics. Not only it put in power BJP for the first time with a thumping majority, but it also drove home interesting anecdotes about the Assam electorate. While anti-incumbency was an important factor after three terms of Congress Government, new permutations and combinations also shaped the election results. BJP succeeded in formulating a rainbow coalition and even reached out to the Muslims who comprise a substantial part of the electorate. For the Muslims also BJP was no more a political pariah and Muslims in many places did vote for BJP. In a report by the Centre for Policy Research, it shows that Muslims are neither a consolidated vote bank nor a monolith. The Muslim electorate is very much complex if not fractured. One of the researchers Bhanu Joshi later commented that in out of the 49 constituencies which have a Muslim majority, BJP won 15 seats showing that Muslims did vote for BJP as well (*IB Times*, May 21, 2016). In another post poll survey carried out by Lokniti for Indian Express, there was anti-incumbency, consolidation of Hindu votes as well as a fracture of Muslim votes which led to the massive victory of BJP (*Indian Express*, May 21, 2016).

Muslims also did not vote en masse as a vote bank for any political party. While it is too early to declare the decline of AIUDF which managed 13 seats and 13% of vote-share, a party exclusive for any religious minority does not seem viable in Assam. AIUDF has further regained some space by taking up issues of D voters especially in the context of the updation of NRC. Nonetheless it remains a fact that Muslims did send a strong message by ensuring the defeat of AIUDF supremo Ajmal. It should be taken in positive stride that politics and elections be played out not on religious and communal lines but on policies.

A look at the performance of AIUDF shows that there is no upsurge of religious nationalism in the form of this party which has been accused time and again of catering to the minority community especially the Muslims of East Bengal origin. AIUDF supremo's brother Sirajuddin Ajmal lost in Barpeta constituency to Congress's Abdul Khaleque which shows that a section of Muslim votes has again rallied behind Congress. While the party has not yet lost its political, electoral significance, it cannot be presumed to be the only choice of the minority community as the minority electorate continues to be split.

Notes

1. Souvenir, Eastern India Muslim Association Convention, 16 October 1977, p. 4.
2. *Ibid.*, p. 5.
3. The 6th General Election to Assam Legislative Assembly, 1971, Statistical Analysis, pp. 19, 32 and 39.
4. Secretary's Report presented at the General meeting held on 10 October 2012, pp. 2-3.
5. Manogya Loiwal, Relief to BJP as Party wins 50% seats in Assam Panchayat Elections, *India Today*, 18 Dec. 2018.
6. Taha Amin Mazumdar, Has BJP really won the Assam Panchayat Polls?, *Newsclick*, 18 Dec. 2018.

References

"Assam Assembly Election 2016 Results: BJP wins in Muslim majority seats, consolidates Hindu votes" published in *International Business Times* on 21st May 2016 and retrieved from https://www.ibtimes.co.in/assam-assembly-elections-2016-results-bjp-wins-muslim-majority-seats-consolidates-hindu-votes-679620

"Lokniti-CSDS post poll analysis: Record Hindu swing in Assam, Cong in decline, States Rising" published in *Indian Express* on 21st May 2016 and retrieved from https://indianexpress.com/article/india/india-news-india/assam-bjp-assembly-elections-results-congress-loss-2811592/

Ahmed, Abu Nasar Saied (2018). *Assam Assembly Elections 2016: Understanding the Choices of Two Communities*, New Delhi: Akanksha Publishing House.

Bhattacharjee, Malini (2016). "Tracing the Emergence and Consolidation of Hindutva in Assam". *Economic and Political Weekly*, 51(16), 80-87, 16 April.

Brass, Paul (1990). *The Politics of India since Independence*. New Delhi: CUP.

Census of India Report, 2011.

Chandra, Kanchan (2005). "Ethnic Parties and Democratic Stability". *Perspectives on Politics*, Vol. 3, No. 2, June.

—— (2017). *Why Ethnic Parties Succeed: Patronage and Ethnic Headcounts in India*. New Delhi: Cambridge University Press.

Dutta, Akhil Ranjan (2017). BJP's Electoral Victory in Assam, 2016: Co-opting the Khilonjiyas. *Social Change*, 47(1), 108-24.

Election Commission Reports of Assembly Elections, 2016.

Election results available at website of Assam State Election Commission.

Guha, Amalendu (1977). *Planters' Raj to Swaraj: Electoral Politics in Assam, 1826-1947*. ICHR.

Jalal, Ayesha (1995). *Democracy and Authoritarianism in South Asia*. Cambridge: CUP.

Joshi, Bhanu, Ashish Ranjan and Neelanjan Sircar (2016). Understanding the Elections in Assam. A Working Paper for *Centre for Policy Research* available at http://www.cprindia.org/research/papers/understanding-election-assam-part-1

Kar, M. (1990). *Muslims in Assam Politics*. New Delhi: Omsons Publications.

Loiwal, Manogya (2018). "Relief to BJP as Party wins 50% seats in Assam Panchayat Elections", *India Today*, 18 Dec.

Mazumdar, Taha Amin. "Has BJP really won the Panchayat Polls?" Newsclick, 18 Dec. 2018.

Misra, Udayon (2016). Victory for Identity Politics, not Hindutva in Assam. *Economic and Political Weekly*, 51(22), 28 May.

Palshikar, Suhas (2003). "The regional parties and democracy: Romantic Rendezvous or Localised Legitimation?" in Ajay Mehra, DD Khanna and Gert W Kueck (eds.) *Political Parties and Party Systems,* New Delhi: Sage.

—— (2004). "Revisiting State Level Parties." *Economic and Political Weekly*, Vol. 39, No. 14/15. April.

Vanaik, Achin (1990). *The Painful Transition: The Bourgeois Democracy of India*. London: Verso Books.

Varshney, Ashutosh (2000). "Is India Becoming More Democratic?" *The Journal of Asian Studies*, Vol. 59, No. 1, Feb.

Weiner, Myron (1978). *Sons of the Soil: Migration and Ethnic Conflict in India*, Princeton: Princeton University Press, p. 124.

Yadav, Yogendra (1996). "The Maturing of Indian Democracy", *India Today*, 31 August.

—— (2000). "Understanding the Second Democratic Upsurge: Trends of Bahujan Participation in Electoral Politics in the 1990s" in Francine R. Frankel (ed.) *Transforming India: Social and Political Dynamics of Democracy*, New Delhi: OUP, pp. 120-45.

Ziegfeld, Adam (2012). "Coalition Government and Party System Change: Explaining the Rise of Regional Political Parties in India". *Comparative Politics*, Vol. 45, No. 1, Oct.

4

Transnational, Postnational or Dual Citizenship: Negotiating Identity by Chakmas of India's Northeast

Konkumoni Boro

I. Introduction

The history of citizenship has been a struggle over how citizenship is to be defined and who should be included and who should be not. This implies citizenship as a very dynamic institution, ever changing and highly contested. Although citizenship is supposed to be perceived in formal legal terms, claiming membership of a nation state with a national identity, but citizenship is not confined to that alone. The idea of citizenship goes beyond from just a formal member of a nation state to membership of multiple nation states with multiple identities, or transnational identity or post-national identity. In the 20th century, citizenship has taken new forms as Jayal puts it, "The history of citizenship in 20th century India is a history of a new way of thinking about the relationship of individuals to the state" (Jayal, 2013). As citizenship laws are highly determined by the divisive legacy of partition, the modern state building process in South Asia after partition have given birth to many "excluded groups" who are either termed as "denizens", or "stateless people", or "aliens" and so on (Baruah, 2003). As demarcating the territories, installing braid wires, erecting fences and posts became a political reality; the state building process in South Asia was accompanied by demographic shifts and massive population transfers. The inevitable consequence of the process of creation of modern nation state in South Asia was that large numbers of people were pushed out of one territory in the pursuit of creation of homogenous nations thereby leading to persecution of many. One such community is the Chakmas of the Chittagong Hill Tracts. The Chakmas make continuous efforts to determine their status, identity, space, and homeland. Their political status and citizenship has been determined by the modern state building process and they still linger with different political status in different parts of the world. Chakmas migrated to India from East Pakistan due to religious atrocities and submergence of their land because of the construction of Kaptai Hydel Dam. One of the host areas of these transborder communities is India's Northeast. The Chakmas have mostly settled in Assam, Arunachal Pradesh, Mizoram and Tripura. Whereas, the Chakmas residing in different parts of India except those in Arunachal Pradesh are legal citizens, in the state of Arunachal Pradesh, they are still lingering as stateless people. Therefore, it becomes imperative to investigate into the case of the Chakmas of India's Northeast, particularly of those in Arunachal Pradesh to explore their citizenship claims over the years of more than five decades of their stay in the state.

II. Research Question

The key research questions that the study aims to address are:

Q: How does a stateless community like the Chakmas negotiate with the ideas of citizenship?

Q: Do Chakmas claim for transnational, postnational or dual citizenship?

III. Methodology

The paper is based on qualitative method of data collection and interpretation. For data collection, in-depth fieldwork was conducted. The paper uses both primary and secondary sources of data. Primary data mostly comprises of observations from the field, in-depth interviews and documents from government offices.

Secondary sources include: books, journal articles, newspapers, government reports and archival documents.

IV. Conceptualizing State Building

In pre-colonial South Asia, modern state building was not introduced and it was a very alien idea to this part of the region. It was a European construct, to demarcate and homogenize nation on regional and cultural lines that may demand for political autonomy (Donnan, 1998). For a long period of time, Europe was characterized by dynastic realms, which was neither unified nor clearly demarcated. Also ancient imperialism aimed at not defining their territories with fixed borders but on controlling people and towns (Paasi, 2005). However, as claimed by Paasi (2005), most of the existing political boundaries were originally created by the European nation-states. The Holy Roman Empire came to an end with the signing in of the Peace of Westphalia in 1648, which also marked the beginning of the modern state system in Europe (Haselsberger, 2014). Subsequently the principle of nation-state sovereignty and the right of national self-determination has slowly emerged and offered a new understanding of frontiers which implied not just dividing people but also territory (*ibid.*). This has resulted to territorialization of borders and demarcation of areas through modern map-making process in Europe. Steadily its application spread to the newly decolonized states in Asia and other regions beyond Europe (Schendel, 1997). Bordering must be considered as a dynamic cultural process, always changing in response to historic development and constantly being transformed by and transforming the social, cultural and political contexts, of the very nature of the limit. Whereas on the one hand, scholars like Haselsberger (2014) reiterates the significance of borders and its clear-cut demarcation, on the other hand Baud and Schendel (1997) argues that national borders are political constructs, which are only imaginary projections of territorial power. The ways borders are projected on the maps are very different from actual consequences in practice (Schendel, 1997). For Haselsberger, 'a world without borders and boundaries is a utopia', as she believes unbounded activities, either economic, social or cultural would be formless. Also administration of a territory would be difficult without clear demarcation. She further argues that in order to attain a national identity, distinction between 'them' and 'us' is of utmost importance (Haselsberger, 2014). However, she also argues that borders change over time and are the result of the bordering process. Haselsberger here ignores the border making process in non-European, noncontiguous areas like the one between India and East Pakistan where states have discontinuous territories. This was an outcome of colonial annexation of the peripheral regions, which Franke (2009) restates as a part of the imperialist policy of expansion to extract resources from these areas (Franke, 2009). As Thongchai Winichakul demonstrated how the foreign concept of map making created the geo-body of Siam although Siam was never directly colonized (Winichakul, 1994). He explains how mapping is a European idea that was imposed on Asian nations. For Siam, mapping was completely an alien concept, which later gave birth to the 'geo-body' of the modern Siam (Winichakul, 1994). Thongchai Winichakul explored the pre-modern nationhood of the preservation of Thainess to the postmodern nationhood of creating a body of the nation. Thongchai Winichakul calls it the 'geo-body' of the nation. Similarly, the colonial rule in the African subcontinent left the society divided on the lines of rural and urban, civilized and uncivilized, citizens and subjects (Mamdani, 1996). Mamdani attempted to show the structural changes that were brought about in the African societies and how the settlers intervened in every aspect of the lives of the natives through direct and indirect intervention. Mamdani saw independence in the African states as the deracialization of the state but not civil society because the reform that came to Africa as a result of independence aimed at deracialization of the civil society but since the rural natives were ruled by customary laws enforcing traditions and customs on tribesman, deracialization did not function there and what it required as Mamdani puts was detribalization. As the reform was limited to only deracialization, the rural sphere remained unchanged (Mamdani, 1996). Mamdani argues that the post-independence reforms had both continuity and change in it. The conservative African states had the continuance of the local tribal heads and the customary laws. In the radical African states, the customary laws were discarded at some places, whereas in some other, single customary were created for all. The attempt here was to develop a uniform, country wide customary law applicable to all peasants regardless of ethnic affiliations. Reformed not to dismantle it totally, but to reorganize the decentralized power and to unify the nation that later led to centralization. Colonization impacts therefore, were not limited only to the period of colonization but in postcolonial period too.

Similarly, James C. Scott's (2010) study of the Zomias reveals that a non-state space exists in the uplands of South East Asia, which was aimed by the modern state to include within the state sphere in the name of uplifting and developing those regions (C. Scott, 2010). Scott termed this procedure as the 'enclosure system.' He argues that by the enclosure method the state attempts to monetize the people and their resources so that they become rentable. Although this process has been styled as development, economic and social progress and integration of the periphery into the social system, but in reality it was an attempt of state intervention into the non-state areas and transform it into fully governed, fiscally productive zones (*ibid.*). Scott argues that the process of state building started with wet rice cultivation. As wet rice cultivation is labor intensive, it requires huge number of population to be engaged in it, which Scott claims as the crucial factor of state making process. Moreover, crops that grow over the ground are easily taxable as they ripen at almost the same time. Therefore, introduction of wet rice cultivation in place of jhum cultivation is seen as an instrument by which state intervened into the non-state areas. Communal economy was transformed into mounting gender and economic differentiation due to excessive state intervention in the economy encouraging the growth of commercial crops by offering incentives to the farmers and discouraging shifting cultivation. This led to the emergence of private property rights in the common property-based societies. The traditional jhum cultivation system was based on certain informal networks and cooperation, sharing of risks, pooling of resources, and mutual insurance system. These traditional methods, according to Verrier Elwin, an eminent British anthropologist upholds democratic ethos, hence should be encouraged (Elwin, 2009). Therefore, unlike Thomas Wilson and Hastings Donnan (1998) who argues that state always exists, for James C. Scott (2010) state building is also a process like nation building, which was absent in some regions before the coming in of the modern state. A total devastation of tribal virtues and tribal society occurs. It also extricates the younger generation from its tribal base.

The British followed a similar policy in Chittagong Hill Tracts (CHT), which Schendel termed as the 'policy of enclosure' by the British. The inhabitants of the Chittagong Hill Tracts have been among worst sufferers of the consequences of the modern state building process. Modern state building in the Indian subcontinent came in the form of territorialization by demarcation of borders, massive population movements and demographic alterations. Territorial partition that happened between India and Pakistan was much more than just drawing imaginary lines on the map. It was about the absolute demographic alteration while restructuring the population as Hindus, Muslims and Sikhs that were transferred from one side to the other. The entire state building process during and after the partition of the Indian subcontinent left profound impact in the lives and memories of the border landers. As in the words of Mishra, border creation "dislocated many and created sufferings for those who lived across the borders" (Mishra, 2014). Same was the case with the Chakmas, an indigenous community in the Chittagong Hill Tracts who were forcefully included in the state of East Pakistan despite their continuous appeal to stay in India. The Chakmas were one of the dominant groups in Chittagong Hill Tracts; to utter dismay, now they have become minorities in their place of origin. The Chakmas' identities are at stake with the drawing and redrawing of the postcolonial India's eastern borders. The Chakmas were subject of the British prior to 14th August 1947 and became citizens of the state of Pakistan thereafter. The identities of Chakmas as citizens of Pakistan changed soon after East Pakistan was separated from West Pakistan and the state of Bangladesh was created in 1971

(K. Singh D., 2010). Those who migrated from East Pakistan due to increasing religious atrocities from the majority Bengali speaking Muslims to India, before the creation of Bangladesh, remained as stateless citizens in India as they are neither accepted as citizens by the Indian state nor they are recognized as citizens by Bangladesh (*ibid.*). Hence, the Chakmas have been deprived of the opportunity to determine their identities and citizenship status.

V. Conceptualizing Citizenship

Jayal envisages that in the process of demarcating the boundaries of the state, the state always leaves out some who are not included within the purview of membership of that territory (Jayal, 2013). The membership into a community is again linked to defining boundaries of a territory. Therefore, Jayal contends that citizenship is not only about states' engagement with their own citizens but also those who are pressing on their borders (*ibid.*). As the territorial boundaries define some as members whereas others as aliens. In India, the idea of citizenship has been largely constructed in the context of partition of 1947 and the nation building effort thereafter. Therefore, although the modern nation state system regulated membership only in terms of one single category i.e. national citizenship but the present era of diversity has given rise to new modalities of membership.

Citizenship, in the Western tradition was first born in the city-states of Greece. In these Greek city-states, citizenship was seen in the form of political participation. As in Aristotle's polis (Aristotle, 1992) political participation was limited only to men. Others like women, slaves, those without property and foreigners were either considered as non-citizens or sub-citizens who were not eligible to become full citizens of the state (Irene Bloemraad, 2008). This is the republican notion of citizenship. Later during the time of Enlightenment, subject hood was seen in the form of Lockean notion of contract and consent whereby members of the state should give away some of their rights to the government by a contract and keeping some rights to themselves. This led to the emergence of what liberals call 'individual rights'. Talking of rights, Marshall put forward a universal notion of citizenship as he posits, "Citizenship is a status bestowed on those who are full members of a community. All who possess the status are equal with respect to the rights and duties with which the status is endowed" (Marshall, 1992). Therefore, Marshall suggests for a universal notion of citizenship where the citizens are full members of political community with civil, political and social rights. While drawing a historical evolution of rights, Marshall advocates that civil rights were the results of economic changes. Although civil rights were universal, political rights were the privilege of limited economic class. However, in the 20th century by the Act of 1918, by adopting manhood suffrage, shifted the basis of political rights from economic substance to personal status.

Till mid of twentieth century, individual was at the core of understanding citizenship and the liberal notion of citizenship perceives citizens as rights bearing individuals where all citizens can equally exercise their rights of citizenship without considering the circumstances of inequality i.e. socio-economic categories like caste, class, gender, nationality, race, etc. This notion of citizenship constitutes an all-inclusive category where all person is equal before the law and no person is legally privileged. Therefore, every individual citizen is seen as possessor of equal rights like right to life, liberty, freedom of speech, conscience, movement and so on. There are no shades in assigning citizenship rights and all enjoy equal rights as all are equal before and in the eyes of law (Jayal, 2013). However, this liberal notion of citizenship has been criticized for overseeing actually existing inequalities. Since nineteen eighties, notions like heterogeneity, plurality, multiculturalism, and difference emerged in understanding the idea of citizenship. As the modern societies began to be recognized as multicultural, the liberal idea of citizenship was under significant criticism. The differences of socio-economic status, race, class, caste, language, etc. that the liberal theory of citizenship ignored; gained prominence under the multicultural and plural society giving rise to the notion of differentiated citizenship. Differentiated citizenship is guaranteed in various institutional forms like minority rights, affirmative actions, language rights, rights to guaranteed representation in governing institutions (Jayal, 2013). Therefore, citizenship is not only about rights and duties of individuals, but also cultural rights of communities. Hence, individuals are perceived as not only citizens but also as part of community and the rights of community. Thus, citizenship is internally conflicting playing two contradictory roles. On the one hand, it is based on the epitome of equality and on the other hand, it legitimizes inequality.

The nation-state model gets more complicated when immigrants of different nationalities enter the territory of the state. In order to protect the minority rights of immigrants, multicultural approach has come up with its definitions of citizenship. Multicultural approach to citizenship upholds group rights, claim for recognition and accommodation of cultural minorities including immigrants (Kymlicka, 1995). And for integration of culturally different minority groups like immigrants, equal citizenship rights are not enough and therefore Kymlicka proposes for 'polyethnic rights' that exempts these groups from laws that disadvantage them (Joppke, 1999). However, critics of multiculturalism claims that it reifies cultural distinctions, making them appear more important than they actually are (Irene Bloemraad, 2008). They feel that multiculturalism aggravates socio-economic and cultural differences.

Scholars have not only observed citizenship as membership within nation state borders but also beyond. This set of literature argues citizenship as membership that goes beyond the territorial borders of a nation state but may be membership of multiple nation states or transnational identities or may be something that is not limited to state but just the mere fact of being humans. This set of literature on transnationalism and postnationalism have critiqued the overemphasis of territorial boundaries to define identity and have responded to the processes of globalization as has given rise to new forms of identity, loyalties and animosities across borders (Isin, 2007). According to these scholars, with globalization there is a decreasing relevance of the state and its sovereignty. They argue that with growing globalization tendencies, citizenship can be seen as transcending nation state borders in line of postnationalism and cosmopolitanism and also citizenship straddling to multiple nations-states giving rise to transnationalism and dual citizenship (Brubaker, 1989; Soysal, 1994; Joppke, 1999). Political cosmopolitanism argues that rights of individuals do not remain confined to nation state borders but transcend national boundaries (Bosniak, 2000). Accordingly, "The new disaggregated concept of citizenship allows individuals to develop and sustain multiple allegiances and networks across state boundaries, in inter as well as transnational context and leads to a cosmopolitanism that can sustain different communities of language, culture, etc." (Chowdhory, 2012).

VI. The Case Study: Chakmas in South Asia

The Chakmas are one of the dominant groups in Chittagong Hill Tracts whose identities and citizenship status are at stake with the drawing and redrawing of the post-colonial India's eastern borders. One reason for selection of this case is due to its continuous change of identity as the Chakmas were subject of the British prior to 14th August 1947 and became citizens of the state of Pakistan thereafter. The identities of Chakmas as citizens of Pakistan changed soon after East Pakistan was separated from West Pakistan and the state of Bangladesh was created in 1971 (K. Singh D., 2010). Those who migrated from East Pakistan due to increasing religious atrocities from the majority Bengali speaking Muslims to India, before the creation of Bangladesh, remained as stateless citizens in India as they are neither accepted as citizens by the Indian state nor they are recognized as citizens by Bangladesh. Hence, Singh claims that the Chakmas has been deprived of the opportunity to determine their identities. The identities of the Chakmas were re constructed when the Chittagong Hill Tracts, which was practically a non-Muslim district, was made a part of Pakistan, although the inhabitants wanted to be a part of the state of India. The Chakmas gained the political identity of the citizen of Pakistan until 1971, when East Pakistan was separated from West Pakistan. Their identities were reconstructed as citizens of Bangladesh.

When after partition, CHT was forcefully made a part of Pakistan, the post-colonial government of Pakistan undertook various policies by which attempts were made to marginalizing the hill people and assimilating them with the mainstream Bengali speaking Muslims. Consequently, the government encouraged migration of plains people who were hitherto restricted from entering the hills during the colonial period; into the sparsely populated hill tracts. These Bengali speaking people comprises of 99% of the total population of Bangladesh and the hill people who the Bengalis refer to as 'primitive', 'wild tribes', are only 1 percent of the total population (Chakma, 1989). Scholars have argued that influx of non-tribal into the hills has been an outcome of a well-planned policy of the government (Talukdar, 1988). Through the policy of development, the government conspired to settle Bengali Muslims in the hills and fluster out the hill tribes people from the Chittagong Hill Tract. As a result, the development projects of establishing more industries, paper mills and hydroelectric projects were carried out. These projects became pull factors for the people from the plains as many job opportunities were created. The lives of the hill people were at stake by these projects as the Kaptai Hydel Electric Project had submerged a vast area inhabited by the Chakmas uprooting many families. These projects were installed with an aim of altering the economy of the uplands from self-sufficient economy to market centered economy. As a result, gradually the chakmas crossed the national borders in search of security and shelter in the Indian states of Mizoram and Tripura. Many were also rehabilitated in Arunachal Pradesh by the Government of India. Those residing in Mizoram and Tripura have attained Indian citizenship but Chakmas of Arunachal Pradesh are still deprived of Indian citizenship rendering them stateless.

VII. Chakmas in Arunachal Pradesh

VII.I. Brief History of the State

Arunachal Pradesh is a state, which is marked by high level of heterogeneity in terms of its culture, tradition, language, religion, dress, food habits and so on. Arunachal Pradesh got its name in 1972, before which it was known by various names;

Frontier Tracts, Backward Tracts, Partially Excluded Areas and North East Frontier Agency (NEFA) (Singh, 1989). The frontier tracts came under the administration of the government of Assam for an interim period of 1947 to 1951. NEFA still continued to be a part of Assam, but its administration was directly controlled by the President of India with the Governor of Assam acting as the agent of the President in delivering his duties. NEFA was elevated to a Union Territory on 21st January 1972 by the North Eastern Areas (Re-organization) Act, 1971. Finally, NEFA emerged as a full-fledged state on 20th February 1987 under the provisions of the State of Arunachal Pradesh Act 1986. The administrative changes have a major role to play in the socio-political status of the Chakmas in Arunachal Pradesh. Of the total population of 10,91,117, according to 2001 census, 63.7 percent constitutes the indigenous population (K. Singh D., 2010). The state is divided into eighteen districts; they are: Papumpare, Changlang, Lohit, West Siang, Tirap, East Siang, Kurung Kumey, West Kameng, Upper Subansiri, Lower Subansiri, East Kameng, Lower Dibang Valley, Tawang, Upper Siang, Anjaw and Dibang Valley, Longding and Namsai (Census, 2011).

VII.II. Settlement of the Chakmas in NEFA

The Chakmas migrated from 1964 to 1969 from erstwhile East Pakistan (present day Bangladesh) to India. The Chakmas, during their migration followed two routes to reach India; one through Tripura and the other through Lushai Hills district (present day Mizoram). As they moved to Assam, the State Government of Assam expressed its incapability to accommodate the Chakmas as many new refugees settled already in Assam. A letter No. GA-71/64 date April 10, 1964, Shri Vishnu Sahay, then Governor of Assam, wrote to then Chief Minister of Assam, Shri P.B. Chaliha regarding the settlement of Chakma refugees in the Tirap frontier division. Another letter No. RHM-24/6410 dated April 27, 1964, Shri A.N. Kidwai, Chief Secretary, Government of Assam, responded and wrote to the Advisor to the Governor of Assam (who was in charge of NEFA) to make necessary arrangements for settlement of

10,000 Chakma refugees. Again in April 21, vide letter No. RR-17/64, the Advisor to the Governor General of Assam, sought proposals from Political Officers for resettlement of refugees along the Indo-China border to strengthen the frontiers and remonstrate China's claim over Arunachal Pradesh and its continuous attempt to occupy Arunachal. As a result, 2,902 Chakma and Hajong families consisting of 14,888 persons were settled in Changlang (former Tirap), Papum Pare (former Subansiri) and Namsai (former Lohit) districts of Arunachal Pradesh in various batches.[1]

VII.III. Rise of the Chakma Problem

In the beginning, at the time of settlement of Chakmas, between 1964-1986, there was no resentment by the locals against the Chakmas. The resentment against the settlers was first disseminated and most powerfully exercised by the AAPSU (All Arunachal Pradesh Students Union), the apex student organization of the state of Arunachal Pradesh. A sudden change in the attitude of the state government and the local population towards the Chakmas was evident in the 80's. In 1980, Chakmas and Hajongs were banned from government services and Chakma and Hajong children from government schools. The ration cards that were given to the Chakmas as refugees were taken away in the 1980's.[2] Therefore, Chakmas are now left in a situation where they can neither avail the benefits of refugees nor the benefits of being citizens, they are left somewhere in between. Chakmas are denied of even birth certificates, hence no domicile, which prevents them from applying in any kind of government jobs. They are also not included in the Public Distribution System (PDS), hence no ration card to buy items at subsidized rates. They are in a state of denial of basic amenities as well as basic rights.

The Chakmas are in an unremitting battle of constructing and reconstructing their identities. For the first time, the resistances and the claims of the Chakmas took an organized under the banner of CCRCAP (Committee for Citizenship Rights of the Chakmas), formed on 2nd October 1991, in New

Delhi. CCRCAP has been continuously struggling to negotiate the identity of Chakmas and Hajongs with the state. Problems with the Chakmas intensified and the situation worsened in 1994 when 'Quit Arunachal' notices were issued by AAPSU to the Chakmas.[3] This was followed by various atrocities on the Chakmas. Due to mounting attacks on the Chakmas, threatening their lives and liberty, the CCRCAP petitioned to the National Human Rights Commission (NHRC) against violation of the human rights of the Chakmas and their forcible eviction. After a writ petition by NHRC to Supreme Court, seeking protection of life and liberty of the Chakmas, the Supreme Court came out with interim directions to the State Government against evicting any "Chakmas through any means which is not in accordance with the law as well as to protect their lives and liberty" on 9th January 1996.[4] The Chakmas of Arunachal Pradesh assert that after the 1996 judgment, a significant change in the attitude of the local communities towards the Chakmas has been noticed. After continuous efforts of the Chakmas, on 3rd March 2004, the Election Commission of India directed the Electoral registration officers in three Assembly Constituencies of 46-Chowkham, 49-Bordumsa-Diyun and 50-Miao of Arunachal Pradesh to include the names of 1497 eligible electors in the electoral rolls to enable them to cast their votes.[5] However, to the dismay of the Chakmas, names of 500 voters were deleted from the electoral rolls. Again the people with a voter id are still deprived of other political and social benefits, like they are not allowed to issue Permanent Resident Certificates. The ambiguities of the status of the Chakmas reveal resentment at the local level against the Chakmas. A milestone was achieved by CCRCAP when on September 17, 2015, Supreme Court delivered the judgment directing the State of Arunachal Pradesh and the Union of India, to finalize the conferment of citizenship rights on eligible Chakmas and Hajongs and also to ensure compliance of directions in judicial decisions referred to in earlier part of this order for protection of their life and liberty and against their discrimination in any manner.[6] The above judgment by the Supreme Court was not implemented until 13th September 2017, when the Home Ministry complied with the 2015

Supreme Court judgment to grant citizenship rights to Chakmas and Hajongs who fled erstwhile East Pakistan in 1964 (Singh, V., 2017). However, the Central Government came up with an idea of 'limited citizenship' for the Chakmas and Hajongs, which means citizenship rights for Chakmas, and Hajongs does not include ownership of land.[7] Here, it should be mentioned that Arunachal Pradesh is a tribal state where land rights are granted only to those who acquires 'Scheduled Tribe' status, which has been denied to Chakmas. This judgment of limited citizenship to Chakmas and Hajongs was declared in order to ensure that "indigenous people's rights won't be diluted," said Minister of State for Home, Kiren Rijiju.[8] Here, citizenship is very ambiguous where it is determined by belonging to a particular state than belonging to an entire country as in some other states like Tripura, Mizoram and Assam, the Chakmas are already recognized as citizens.

VII.IV. Chakmas' Negotiation for Citizenship: Transnational, Postnational or Dual

Citizenship is not only about legal right to belong but also a moral sense of belonging to a place and its community. Convergence of both legal and moral right, results in a sense of legitimate citizenship, making an individual feel both legally entitled and morally engaged (Mitra, 2010). In absence of any one will lead to either a condition where legal citizenship lacks a sense of identification to the soil or a situation where there is primordial attachment to the land with no legal sanction. However, there might also be situations when one might not be aware of their legal entitlement or even if aware, may not have possessions of rights and benefits generates more meaningful citizenship, or one might reject the legal rights of citizenship and get motivated by some innate force of loyalty towards a different authority other than the national state.

There are various factors, which may influence identities, and in case of migrants, the policies of integration undertaken by the receiving states may largely determine migrant identities (Ruud Koopmans, 2005). Receiving states may directly impact migrant identities by offering and labeling new categories of identification like foreigners, asylum seekers, illegal immigrant, refugees, ethnic minority and so on which were previously unidentified in the state of origin. Similarly, in the case of the Chakmas, it has been noticed that identities assigned by the receiving state has time and again constructed the identity with which the Chakmas identify themselves. As in Arunachal Pradesh, although the Chakmas consider themselves as 'locals' of the state as most of them are either born there or those who had migrated, it has been more than five decades now. Yet, the continuous labeling of the Chakmas as 'refugees' both by the government and the other ethnic communities of the state have created a subconscious self-identification of 'refugee' among the Chakmas who identify the other neighboring communities as 'locals'. The Chakmas are not seen identifying themselves as 'locals' neither do they identify the *Deoris* and *Ahoms* residing at Diyun circle as 'locals' despite the fact that they are Indian citizens. The *Deoris* and *Ahoms* are believed to have migrated from the neighboring state of Assam. Another blotch on their identity of not identifying as 'locals' have emerged from the fact that they have not been assigned the status of 'tribals' and thereby excluding them from the Arunachal Pradesh Scheduled Tribe Status (APST).

It should also be noted that migrants or refugees also do not arrive with just one identity but several competing, cross cutting and overlapping ones. Like the Chakmas see themselves as not only Chakmas but also Buddhist, minorities, Indians; whereas again others may perceive them as refugees, illegal immigrants, Bangladeshis or Pakistanis. Furthermore, postnational and transnational theorists have argued that in the wake of a highly globalized and interconnected world, has given rise to new forms of identity, loyalties and animosities across borders (Isin, 2007). Soysal explains on the basis of her work on guest workers of post-war Europe that citizenship is not a matter of concern for the immigrant guest workers who can attain safe membership status without becoming citizens (Soysal, 1994). So, here the scholar has detached membership from citizenship. This gives rise to a new form of 'post national membership' where the members strive for not a national belonging but belonging to a world of universal human rights that goes beyond national citizenship (*ibid.*). Transnational theorists again argue that migrants may strive for dual citizenship where they identify themselves as strongly to their state of origin as much to the state of settlement. Lack of strong identification with the country of residence and occasions to powerfully improve their condition, in such cases, migrants will parallel the state's rejection of them by staying strongly connected to their countries of origin (Ruud Koopmans, 2005). Surprisingly, unlike what the transnational scholars have argued, the case of the Chakmas revealsa strong sense of belonging to their place of residence and to their place of origin. Their claims for citizenship as a status, rights and benefits do not transcendent Indian national identity. However, variances in such claims are also conditioned by the factor if one has migrated or was born in the place of residence. Much stronger sense of 'Indianness' is observed among the youth, mostly who are born in India. Those belonging to older generation, particularly those who migrated from erstwhile East Pakistan, still refer to CHT as their *'Desh'* but do not claim for political membership or citizenship of the state of Bangladesh. Dual identity plays a role in the case of the Chakmas, not crossing the national boundary of India but within its borders. Many a times, the Chakmas from the state of Arunachal Pradesh refrains from identifying themselves from the same state but from any other state of the country just to liberate themselves from the stigma of 'refugees' that has been associated with the Chakmas from the state of Arunachal Pradesh. Instead, they prefer to identify with other Chakmas inhabiting state like Tripura or Mizoram where the Chakmas are not only citizens of the country but also are recognized as 'scheduled tribes'. Therefore, it has been observed that although the Chakmas have identified themselves with multiple identities from time to time yet their claims for citizenship remains intensely confined to that of India, i.e. their place of residence.

VIII. Conclusion

The case of the Chakmas is a classic case of colonial gaffe and postcolonial modern state building process. In the present-day context, where the whole nation is grappling with the questions of immigration, citizenship, rights and the debates on inclusion-exclusion; it becomes imperative to delve deeper into the causes of such population flows as well as its consequences. It also becomes significant to see how these 'excluded' communities perceive 'membership,' 'rights,' and 'identity'. This paper has been a sincere attempt to provide a holistic picture of modern state building process and its impact on some of the borderland communities like the Chakmas. This paper argues that borders and territories are significant determining factors in one's citizenship status and identity as in the context Asia, borders are still strictly regulated and citizenship is still strictly linked to one's territory. And as long as state is the guarantor of rights, it is unrealizable that it would act as a guarantor of citizens with multiple, transnational and postnational citizenship claims.

Notes

1. See the 105th Rajya Sabha Report of the Committee of Petitions, for details and the 7th Report on Committee on Petitions (Tenth Lok Sabha).
2. *Ibid.*
3. See Committee for Citizenship Rights of the Chakmas and Hajongs of Arunachal Pradesh (CCRCHAP), 'CCRCHAP: Celebrating 25 Years of Community Service', Diyun, Changlang District, Arunachal Pradesh.
4. National Human Rights Commission v. State of Arunachal Pradesh and another, p. 5.
5. See the Order by the Election Commission of India, No. 23/ARUN/2003, March 3, 2004, p. 41.
6. See Committee for CCRCHAP & Others vs. State of Arunachal Pradesh & Others, Supreme Court, 17 September 2015.
7. PTI, 'Government to Grant Citizenship to Chakmas,' *The Wire*, September 13, 2017 retrieved on December 24, 2017.
8. TNN, 'Centre Grants Citizenship on Chakma-Hajong Refugees,' *The Times of India*, September 14, 2017 retrieved on December 24, 2017.

References

Aristotle. *Politics.* London: Penguin, 1992.

Baruah, Sanjib. "Citizens and Denizens: Ethnicity, Homelands and the Crisis of Displacement in Northeast India." *Journal of Refugee Studies*, 2003.

Bosniak, Linda. "Citizenship Denationalized." *Indiana Journal of Global Legal Studies*, 2000.

Brubaker, William Rogers. "Membership Without Citizenship: The Economic And Social Rights of Noncitizens." In *Immigration and the Politics of Citizenship in Europe and North America*, by William Rogers Brubaker, 145-62. University Press of America, 1989.

C. Scott, James. *The Art of Not Being Governed.* New Delhi: Orient Blackswan Private Limited, 2010.

Chakma, Syed Aziz-al Ahsan and Bhumitra. "Problems of National Integration in Bangladesh: The Chittagong Hill Tracts." *Asian Survey* (University of California Press) 29 (1989): 959-970.

Chakravarty, Ipshita. *Scroll.in.* September 17, 2017. https://scroll.in/article/850801/what-does-limited-citizenship-mean-for-chakma-refugees-in-arunachal-pradesh.

Chowdhory, Nasreen. "Assessing "Belonging" and Claims of "Home" among Refugees: A Note on Repatriation in South Asia." *Peace Prints: South Asian Journal for Peacebuilding*, 2012.

Donnan, Thomas M. Wilson and Hasting. *Border Identities: Nation and State at International Frontiers.* Cambridge University Press, 1998.

Elwin, Verrier. *A Philosophy for NEFA.* New Delhi: Isha Books, 2009.

Franke, Marcus. *War and Nationalism in South Asia: The Indian State and the Nagas.* New York: Routledge, 2009.

Haselsberger, Beatrix. "Decoding borders. Appreciating border impacts on space and people." *Planning Theory and Practice* (Routledge), 2014: 505-26.

Irene Bloemraad, Anna Korteweg and Gokce Yurdakul. "Citizenship and Immigration: Multiculturalism, Assimilation, and Challenges to the Nation-State." *The Annual Review of Sociology*, 2008: 153-79.

Isin, Engin F. "Theorizing Acts of Citizenship." In *Acts of Citizenship*, by Engin F. Isin and Greg M. Nielsen. Chicago: Zed books, 2007.

Jayal, Niraja Gopal. *Citizenship and its Discontents: An Indian History.* Ranikhet: Permanent Black, 2013.

Joppke, Christian. "How immigration is Changing Citizenship: A Comparative View." *Ethnic and Racial Studies* (Routledge), 1999: 629-52.

K. Singh, Deepak. *Stateless in South Asia.* New Delhi: Sage, 2010.

——. *Stateless in South Asia: The Chakmas between Bangladesh and India.* New Delhi: Sage, 2010.

Kymlicka, Will. *Multicultural Citizenship: A Liberal Theory of Minority Rights*. New York: Clarendon Press: Oxford, 1995.

Mamdani, Mahmood. *Citizen and Subject: Contemporary Africa and the legacy of late colonialism*. New Jersy: Princeton University Press, 1996.

Marshall, T.H. *Citizenship and Social Class*. London: Pluto Press, 1992.

Mishra, Deepak K. "Developing the Border: The State and the Political Economy of Development in Arunachal Pradersh." In *Borderland Lives in Northern South Asia*, by David N. Gellner, 141-62. New Delhi: Orient Blackswan, 2014.

Mitra, Subrata. "Citizenship in India: Some Preliminary Results of a National Survey." *Economic and Political Weekly*, 2010: 46-53.

Paasi, Anssi. "The Changing Discourses on Political Boundaries: Mapping the backgrounds contexts and contents." In *B/ordering Space*, by Olivier Kramsch and Wolfgang Zierhofer Henk Van Houtum, 17-31. Ashgate Publishing Limited, 2005.

Ruud Koopmans, Paul Statham, Marco Giugni anf Florence Passy. *Contested Citizenship: Immigration and Cultural Diversity in Europe*. London: University of Minnesota Press, 2005.

Schendel, Michiel Baud and Willem Van. "Toward a Comparative History of Borderlands." *Journal of World History* (University of Hawai Press), 1997: 211-42.

Singh, Chandrika. *Emergence of Arunachal Pradesh as a State*. Delhi: Mittal, 1989.

Singh, Vijayta. "Why is it difficult to grant citizenship to Chakmas." September 23, 2017.

Soysal, Yasemin Nuhoglu. *Limits of Citizenship: Migration and Postnational Membership in Europe*. The University of Chicago Press, 1994.

Talukdar, S.P. *The Chakmas: Life and Struggle*. Delhi: Gian Publishing House, 1988.

Winichakul, Thongchai. *Siam Mapped: A History of the Geo body of a Nation*. Honolulu: University of Hawaii Press, 1994.

5

The Role of Maibi in Safeguarding the Tradition of Manipur

Anuradha Nongmaithem

Introduction

The present Manipur is the result of assimilation of tedious territorial conflicts over years among the ethnic kingdoms over supremacy. The existence of Manipur is always under the threat from its inception. It has passed through the prehistoric, ancient and medieval phase, and has come a long way since then. Manipur is a breathtaking paradise on earth and many tourists who visited the place have validated its beauty and distinctive specialty. The place is surrounded by nine beautiful hills as if nature is protecting its beauty from outside people and intruders. The plain valley is where the Meitei indigenous dwell, and in the hills the other indigenous tribes dwell. They have lived in harmony as brothers and sister from its inception until its exposure to the outside world. The conflict and tension between two dwellers started with the coming of the outside people in Manipur. Since its merger to the newly independent India in 1949, the tension between the communities has also intensified. We cannot go back and change the past but the disagreement between different indigenous groups mounted up and several other issues also cropped up in Manipur which has rapidly changed from bad to worse. It has come a long way since then without much significant achievement. Imphal is the capital of Manipur, and it is one of the seven sisters of north eastern India. The neighboring states of Manipur are Nagaland to the north, Mizoram to the south and Assam to the west and it shares its border with the country Myanmar to its east. Manipur is also known as Kangleipak or Meiteileibak. Kh Ratan Kumar Singh is his book *Lai Haroba of Manipur: Indigenous Festival of the Meitei* has elaborately discussed about the origin of Manipur. The passage below gives information of how the name came into being and how it was before Hinduism came to Manipur,

> Manipur is a term given to this land after the declaration of Hinduism as a state religion during the time of the great ruler of Manipur, Pamheiba or Garibaniwaz, in the beginning of the eighteenth century. In the early times, she had different indigenous names such as Tillikoktong Ahanba in Hayi Chak, Mira-Pongthoklam in Haya Chak, Hanna Semba Konna Loiba in Khunung Chak and Muwapali Mayai Sumtongpanin early Konna (Langba) Chak. In the later ages of Konna (Langba) Chak, it was popularly known as Kanglei Pungmayol, Kangleipak and Meitrabak. (S. Ratan Kumar, 1)

It is important to note that Manipur was in the continuous process of transformation and the process is still going on with the assimilation of Hinduism and changes from one stage to another till date. Hinduism entered into the concept in Manipur during the "second half of the fifteen century" (S. Ratan Kumar, 37). With the coming of Hinduism in Manipur, typical indigenous way of life has been disturbed in many ways.

In a book entitled, *Dance Music and Ritual in Manipur* by Byron Aihara, she has done a detail study of Lai Haraoba. In the introduction of the book, she explores the origin of the settlers of Manipur. It says that, "The historical written records of the Meitei chronicle the existence of a complex monarchic society dating back 2,000 years, which represented the unification of the proto-Meitei under the first king named Pakhangba" (3). This proves that Meitei has a long history of its existence with written record and details over 2000 years old. Currently the border issues between Myanmar and Manipur is creating havoc and tension among the people of Manipur. The NSCN (National Socialist Council of Nagaland) demanding to create Greater Nagaland, by taking land from Manipur is mounting tension among different communities with the politician of the state acting as a mute spectator. Manipur has a long history of 2000 years old, yet the center seems to be quite blind to all the issues occurring in Manipur. The continuous conflicts have impacted many lives and hampered growth in Manipur. The arm conflict in the states with its age old insurgency movement has destroyed many families and claimed many innocent lives too. When will all these war come to an end? What is the purpose of all this fight at the cause of one's life? Is it worth shedding blood? What we all are yearning for is peace and co-existence? The next questions that's comes to one's mind are, "Is it harmful to have desire to safeguard one's own identity and culture?" Should one sacrifice everything in the name of making one nation? Is it fair on the part of the mainland politician to take away everything from the indigenous? How about bridging the huge gap and working on common goal of betterment and co-existence? Why is there need to convert everything in the context of Hindu or Hindutva?

The culture and tradition which has been in practice for centuries play a significant role in shaping the national idea of the particular state and ultimately of the whole nation if we are going to talk about India in the larger context. Other countries have less issues with regards to one nation, one religion, one family but it might sound superficial in India since India is a diverse land with various sub-cultures, traditions and different languages. And I believe every community would like to protect one's own culture and tradition and the people responsible for policy making must take serious effort to preserve it. But in the process of preserving one's own tradition I do also agree that it should not hamper the growth of the larger context that is India as a whole. Every individual in the country love being an Indian, even the Meiteis also feel proud to be an Indian but not to the extent that in being Indian we will be robbed naked of our native culture, land and tradition. The basic fact that Manipuri are different from the rest of the mainland, the constitution and the political leader at the center should by any means give protection and safeguard its unique identity in real sense rather than providing mere lip-service.

In an article entitled, "If George Orwell were alive today, he would consider both Islamism and Hindutva as versions of nationalism" from a web source states that:

> A nationalist is one who thinks solely, or mainly, in terms of competitive prestige.... His thoughts always turn on victories, defeats, triumphs and humiliations. He sees history, especially contemporary history, as the endless rise and decline of great power units, and every event that happens seems to rise and decline of great power units, and every event that happens seems to him a demonstration that his own side is on the upgrade and some hated rival is on the downgrade. Thus wrote George Orwell, one of the most intellectually independent commentators of the 20th century in a 1945 essay.

The passage above is relevant to ponder and to re-think "What is actually nationalism or nation?" India is literally going through a tough phase defining the term nation. There are also claims of certain political party trying to convert India into Hindu nation. This sounds superficial and hypocritical. "Who is a national? Who is a true nationalist?" I believe everyone in their true sense loves their own nation to which they belongs.

Keeping in mind the ever changing scenario of nation and nationalism the paper is mostly going to focus on how indigenous culture and tradition is safeguarded by the Maibi in Manipur. How the tradition is passed on from one generation to another without any discontinuity for centuries. The tradition and culture that we see now in Manipur is assimilation of Hinduism and Meiteism. In spite of all this assimilation and amalgamation, the Meiteis are able to preserve some of its age old typical scared practice till date and Lai Haraoba is one of them. The paper is an attempt to put forward the idea that India is a land of diverse culture and tradition, and each community has its own right to preserve as well as safeguard its own tradition. The sentiment and emotion of a nation is a strong feeling and personal. The world had witnessed several war and bloodshed in the name of nation making and nationalism. What have we all learnt from these wars? Absolutely nothing! We are still following the footstep of our ancestor and the cold war among communities is still alive and vibrant. The paper focus only on how the maibi of Manipur carries on the task of safeguarding the tradition, preserving its indigenous values in spite of the external forces that try to destroy the integrity of Manipur. As Anthony Smith rightly put in, "that one should not consider nations as solely the product of the modern revolutions of the west which destroyed the Agrarian empires. Modern nations also developed on the basis of pre-existing ethnic identity" (*The Ethnic Origins of Nations* by Anthony D. Smith, 415). The per-existing ethnic identity is what makes a place and its people unique and different from others.

Becoming National: A Reader edited by Geoff Eley and Ronald Grigor Suny gives detail of how "ethnic communities" have same syndrome. It says,

(1) a common name for the unit of population included;
(2) a set of myth of common origins and descent for that population;
(3) some common historical memories of things experienced together;
(4) a common "historic territory" or "homeland", or an association with one;
(5) one or more element of common culture-language, customs, or religion;
(6) a sense of solidarity among most members of the community. (109-10)

The above points reflect the condition of Manipur as these distinctive features are relevant to the Meitei. The Meiteis are able to maintain ethnic culture and tradition through ages without sacrificing essence of its origin in the ever changing modern world. It in this context the few following paragraphs will discuss the role of Maibi, how for centuries they are able to retain the old tradition and customs which ultimately have safeguarded it for the future generation.

Role of Maibi

Manipuri society and community was "organized through the concept of blood relationship and kin, women were closely associated with the source of power in the center", says Salam Irene in her book *Women of Manipur: An Alternative Perspective* (13). Women in Manipur have always enjoyed certain status from the rest of the other women in the country. Meitei women are highly spiritual and hard worker. They are by nature traditionalist and have a keen love for its culture and custom. They play a significant role in some religious rituals and practices. Majority of the Meiteis in Manipur are Hindus. Manipuri in particular follow traditional deities in spite of the impact of modernity. In true sense the Meiteis have not given up their age old tradition and way of life in many ways. Many Meitei have assimilated into the Hindu way of worshipping but still the spirit of native worshipping is very much alive till today. It is in this context, the role of Maibi and Amaibi are important in keeping the tradition alive. Lai Haraoba is a typical indigenous festival of Manipur and Maibis and Amaiba are main protagonists of the festival. Maibi culture of Manipur is closely related to *Sanamahisn (a pre-Hindu religion of Manipur)* which has been continuing till date without being compromised to any external forces that try to destroy Manipur and its integrity. The philosophy and the practices are closely associated with animistic faith in nature. It idolizes and rejoices female spirituality. The maibis are the traditional priestess and maiba are the priest but they are not a separate caste in Manipuri society, but part of the community. In the book entitled *Rituals, Politics and Power in North East India: Contextualising the Lai Haraoba of Manipur* by Otojit Kshetrimayum in the chapter "Maibi Culture and Lai Haraoba: Interrogating Women's Religious Authority and Autonomy" the author explains the genesis of maibi in details. And the maibi are categorized into three types:

1. The priestess,
2. The mid-wife, and
3. The healers.

The maibis in general trained themselves in dance, music and the ritual form under a strict supervision called *Ima* (mother)

Guru over a period of time. The maibis are taken as the chosen ones to connect the human to the supernatural world. Their food habits and dress are different from the common women. They usually wear white colour attire. The mid-wife maibis are also known as "Wangon Shangda Angangbu Ngaibi Maibi", as the name suggested their main job is to help in delivering the baby and to cut the umbilical cord. The healers' maibis acts as shamans and as medicine men; they look after the health related issues and they also especially help people fight the evil spirits and are able to treat aliment using traditional medicine.

Space play an important role for the celebration of Lai Haraoba. First and foremost, and foremost it need an open space, and all the dance, songs and ritual are performed in the space where all the spectators can clearly observe what is going on. The festival lasts for few days sometimes over a week too, and the festival starts with the coming of the lais (gods) on the day one till the returning of the lais (gods) on the final day of the festival. On the day one the maibi called forth the lais from the water known as ikouba (calling of the lais) and the day's long ceremony starts from that very moment. In the book *The Pleasing of the Gods: Meitei Lai Haraoba* Saroj N. Arambam Parratt and John Parratt in the introductory chapter have elaborately explained the main rituals of the Lai Haraoba. It says:

(1) The *Laibou (birth)* cycle consists of a dance sequence depicting creation, an invitation to sexual congress, the creation lyric (anoirol), and a mimed dance with antiphonal singing demonstrating the life-cycles;

(2) The Panthoibi cycle, a series of lyrics largely to do with fertility;

(3) A third cycle, performed beneath a canopy (*Phijang*), consisting of complex dances, accompanied by songs, which are meant to portray the creation of the universe; and

(4) On the last day only, a series of dance and lyrics which symbolise the gathering in of the universe into one (*Ougri*) and ending in a song of rejoicing (*Kencho*). (Parratt, 21)

The above series is similar for all the Lai Haraoba celebration everywhere in Manipur. Apart from these four several other activities accompanied the festival like offering flowers and fruits to the deities. The maibi predicts oracles to the people who want to know their future, followed by numerous rituals of cleaning of the particular community where the Lai Haraoba festival is held. The main pivotal of every Lai Haraoba is the Laibouchongba. These are the systematic dance step or sequence. It is well choreographed cycle of dance and songs performed by maiba, maibi and the penakhongba. It depicts the creation of the land from a vast formless water body and inception of life, evolving into plant life, fish, animals and ultimately human beings. One dance sequence consists of 64 movements which is the formation of human parts. The Lai Haraoba is an overall cycle of how human should live on earth and the main theme of the Lai Haraoba is the celebration of fertility and continuation of cycle of life on earth. All these pre-historic ritual is still preserved even today.

The maibis and maibas are main functionaries of the Lai Haraoba rituals. There are series of rituals that are performed during the weeklong festival. Maibi's dance formed is the base of all the dance form of Manipur. "In Manipur, there is the close association of religion with religious dance and music" (Otojit, 89), Lai Haraoba is a unique and distinctive presentation of Manipuri culture and custom. It is the unique narration of creation, cycle of birth and death on earth in its finest presentation through songs and dance movement which is passed on from one generation to another. There are many studies which reveal that maibi occupied a high-status during king's rule in Manipur, "A maibis's oracular power has tremendous effect on the audience and sometimes exerts far-reaching influence upon the society" (Otojit, 90). The duties of maibis can be summed up as:

(i) Chanting the rituals in honour of the deities.

(ii) They are the medium between the worshiper and the deities.

(iii) They direct the ritualistic process in the festival.

(iv) The ancient songs are preserved through them.

(v) They involved the community men and women thereby imparting rituals and customs.

(vi) They are the custodian of sacred traditional knowledge.

(vii) They are the people with unexplained power and possess the gift of foreseeing things.

With the changing scenario and the unstable political situation in Manipur, women equally take part in protecting the state integrity from the external forces that wanted to destroy Manipur. The crucial role played by the Maibi cannot be underestimated. They have been following the pattern taught by their teachers and they keep imparting important message of indigenous culture and tradition. The passage below says that:

> A nation is a named community of history and culture, possessing a unified territory, economy, mass education system and common legal rights. I take this definition from the ideals and blueprints of generations of nationalists and their followers. It sums up an "ideal type" of the nation that is fairly widely accepted today, even if given units of population aspiring to be full nations in this sense, lack one or other of these characteristics in lesser or greater degree. For example, in a unit of population aspiring to constitute a full nation, certain categories of the population may be excluded from the full exercise of the common legal rights. Or they may not enjoy equal access to the common system of education, or equal mobility in the territorial economy. (*Becoming National: A Reader*, 107-08)

Manipur was a separate nation with separate identity with its specific rules and regulation until its merger. Things drastically changed in terms of border-boundary, assimilation of new rules and regulation, with AFSPA (Arms Forces Special Power Acts, 1958), social unrest, insurgency, killings, extortions, kidnapping border conflict with Myanmar and other neighboring states, to name a few. In spite of this chaotic situation the indigenous culture is still intact due to the conscious effort by the people of Manipur, especially the maibis. The role and the duty of maibi is unique in preserving the unique indigenous tradition for centuries. It is believed that the ritual of the Lai Haraoba is one of the most scared and vital elements for the existence of the Meitei people. According to David Kertzer, "...ritual has always been and will continue to be an essential part of political life, used to symbolize, simplify and enhance political messages" (Otojit Kshetrimayum, 96).

Conclusion

The history of fighting for one's nation dates back to several centuries. The impulse of nationalist feelings have been so strong among many groups that they are not only willing to kill but are also willing to die for their nation. It is one of the fundamental sentiments that hold members of an imagined community with the single thread of either religion or cultural or ethnic identity. These identities are further strengthened with a political principle of sovereignty. The nation in modern times has a strong territorial component.

It "guarantee the existence of a nation, to preserve its distinct identity, and to provide a territory where the national culture and ethos are dominant", then why is that the Meitei feel threatened of being wiped off totally in the name of making one nation.

Perhaps the core question about nationalism, especially in the context of India is a bit ambiguous. There are various aspects that need to be kept in mind. With the ever increasing concept of one nation, one family where all the people of the world unites as one global family, will it be wise trying to safeguard indigenous culture and custom, time will only answer. Few things that I would like to ponder are to understand each unique heritage and give freedom to exercise their age old tradition which the future generation will cherish. It takes benevolence and good leaders to respect each one of us on this planet earth. There are different views regarding theories of nationalism. In an article "Gastronomy or geology? The role of nationalism in the reconstruction of nations" by Anthony D. Smith in the conclusion of the article, he gave different perspectives of nationalism from different theories. It says that, "As for the nationalist the 'past is clear and unproblematic'". The role of the nationalist is just to remind the people of its glorious past which was always in the psyche of the community. He further emphasizes that to the perennialists, nation is "immemorial". Nation might change and transform itself and build on new nation based on their ethnic identity, 'but the identity of a nation is unchanging'. According to the modernist past is not relevant. 'It is a modern phenomenon'. The whole concept of nation has flourished because of the 'industrial society'. To the post-modernist, 'past is more problematic'. They do agree that it is a modern cultural condition and there will be mixed traditions for the quest for the imagined political community. All the theories that are discussed above have its own loopholes. The lingering question on nationalism still remains unanswered. There is no doubt that people sharing the same culture and tradition do have an undeniable sense of belonging to each other and sense of solidarity towards the place they lived together. The whole discussion is left to only one issue, how are we going to look at the larger concept of nation. Although Laiharaoba witnessed some decline due to political situation, insurgency movements, Sharmila's hunger strike against AFSPA in Manipur, but in the recent times it has increased tremendously. There is a strong sense of reviving the lost religion like Sanamahism, Meiteism, and there is an attempt to replace the Bengali script with the Meitei script as well. The age old practice gives the Meitei a sense of pride and sense of belongingness to the land called Manipur. The idea of one Nation will stand strong only when the indigenous practices get its due recognition and protection like other traditional practice of the mainland. This will ultimately contribute towards the building of a harmonious nation i.e. India.

References

Aihara, Byron. *Dance Music and Ritual in Manipur*. Nepal: Vajra Books, 2016.

Becoming National: A Reader edited by Geoff Eley and Ronald Grigor Suny http://jan.ucc.nau.edu/~sj6/SmithOriginsNations.pdf

Irene, Salam. *Women of Manipur: An Alternative Perspective*. New Delhi: Akansha Publishing House, 2014.

"If George Orwell were alive today, he would consider both Islamism and Hindutva as versions of nationalism" https://www.thehindu.com/opinion/columns/the-features-of-a-nationalist/article24241737.ece

Kshetrimayum, Otojit. *Rituals, Politics and Power in North East India: Contextualising the Lai Haraoba of Manipur*. New Delhi: Ruby Press & Co., 2014.

Parratt, Saroj Nalini Arambam and John Parratt. *The Pleasing of the Gods: Meitei Lai Haraoba*, Imphal: Jain Book Shop, 2018.

Singh, Ratan Kumar. *Lai Haraoba of Manipur: Indigenous Festival of the Meitei*. 2nd Edition. Imphal: Padma Printers, 2019.

Smith, D. Anthony. "Gastronomy or geology? The role of nationalism in the reconstruction of nations". https://www.sneps.net/t/images/Articles/Smith_1995.pdf

——. "The Ethnic of Origins of Nations". http://library.mpib-berlin.mpg.de/toc/z2010_581.pdf

6

The Need for Socially Achieved Inclusive Nationalism Against Ethno-Nationalism: A Select Study of Easterine Kire's *Bitter Wormwood* and Arupa Patangia Kalita's *Felanee*

Apurba Borbora and Urbashi Borbora

Introduction

Nationalism is an ideology that has led the process of nation-building and also the world wars. Its premises differ according to the goals of a nation. Nationalism can be categorized as civic or ethnic, inclusive or exclusive. "Civic nationalism, founded on the values of liberty and justice, is underpinned by social contract theory…" (Kathleen Kerr, *Literary Theory and Criticism*, 362). Ethnic-nationalism, also known as ethno-nationalism, is the sense of bond between people sharing ethnic ancestry, heritage, culture and language. Nationalism is often regarded as exclusive for, individuals of a nation tend to define themselves in terms of 'who they are not'. But a nation with diversity and internal conflicts needs an inclusive version of nationalism. In India, there is a need for racial unity, for overcoming caste distinctions. India consists of people belonging to different ethnic groups, castes and races which raise the issue of separatist sub-nationalism. As said by Tagore in his lecture "Nationalism in the West",

> Her mission has been like that of a hostess to provide proper accommodation to her numerous guests whose habits and requirements are different from one another.

> It is giving rise to infinite complexities whose solution depends not merely upon tactfulness but sympathy and true realization of the unity of man. (Tagore, *Nationalism*, 15-16)

India should, therefore, move towards such version of inclusive nationalism where people are united by feelings of sympathy and not ethno-nationalism that ultimately creates conflict. Inclusive nationalism is achieved politically, culturally and socially. "Our real problem in India is not political. It is social", says Tagore in his lecture "Nationalism in India" (Tagore, *Nationalism*, 117). This need for socially achieved inclusive nationalism is projected in Easterine Kire's novel *Bitter Wormwood* and Arupa Patangia Kalita's *Felanee* (originally written in Assamese and translated into English by Deepika Phukan as *The Story of Felanee*). People of Assam and Nagaland have faced insurgency for many years when, inspired by sense of ethno-nationalism, many rebel groups had called for separate, sovereign nation. The two selected novels portray the condition of people during those years of conflict. The characters of the novel such as Neibou and Felanee, represent the yearnings of people in general. They, having faced the horrors of communal and ethnic clash, long for peaceful survival.

Discussion

I

Easterine Kire's novel spans from 1937 to 2007 that is around seventy years. The novel begins with the birth of Moseline, also referred as Mose, in 1937 and ends with his death in 2007. Mose joins the Naga struggle for independence along with his friend Neitou in 1956. The people of the Naga Hills had been claiming for a separate nation since the colonial British Government was investigating the transition to Indian independence and planning to include them within India. In 1929, the Naga Club submitted a memorandum to the Simon Commission to state that the Nagas should be excluded from the coming political reforms in India, and that the Nagas—who were neither Hindu nor Muslim—should not be made part of the Indian union (Appendix I, *Bitter Wormwood*, 244). In the Memorandum they mentioned, "We have no unity among us and it is only the British Government that is holding us together now" (Appendix II, *Bitter Wormwood*, 248).

> The conflict which began as peaceful resistance turned into a violent war after the death of Mahatma Gandhi. He had supported the Naga right to remain independent of India. However, the government of free India chose the path of military aggression to make the Nagas submit. When the military oppression reached its highest point in 1956, the Naga Army came into existence.

Kire traces the rise of factionalism and gradual decline of Naga struggle through the life of Mose. But there is also a hope for stable and peaceful future towards the end of the novel when Mose's grandson, Neibou meets and becomes friend with Rakesh, the boy from mainland India.

In 'ethnic nationalism', ancestry and language determine national identity. The Nagas were driven by ethno-nationalism to fight for freedom from India. Mose and Neitou become a part of this freedom struggle at the age of nineteen in the novel. An officer of the Naga Underground says, "The Indians may have more men and more guns, but this is our ancestral land to which we are bonded. The Indian soldier does not feel for the land as we do. Sooner or later we will defeat them" (*Bitter Wormwood*, 95).

The battle between the Indian Army and the Naga Underground made the ordinary people of Nagaland suffer a lot. Villages were burnt, people were tortured and killed. In 1963, when Nagaland was made the state of the Indian Union and a 'Cease-fire' was being negotiated between Indian Government and the Naga Underground, Mose retired from the Underground. But the problem of the Naga people was yet to be solved. Meanwhile, factional killings begun by breakaway groups erupted in the Naga National Council, eroding the Naga cause through the years. Factionalism "made Nagas kill their fellow Nagas" (*Bitter Wormwood*, 212). Mose was accidentally killed by members of such a factionalist group. Mose's grandson,

Neibou, who had often despaired over the situation of his people, seemed to lose faith completely after Mose's death. However, he comes to a solution for the Naga problem while discussing it with his friend, Rakesh and Rakesh's mother, Dipti—that is of detaching oneself, deconstructing history (*Bitter Wormwood*, 235-37).

The Nagas are known for their warrior ancestry. They have "a traditional history of 1700 years as a free and independent nation which had never been interrupted" (Sanyu, 24). So, they had a long period of conflict with India for their own land. But clinging to a history of conflict often kills solutions, stops progress and deteriorates the present. As said by Neibou in the novel, "The trouble with us Nagas is that we have allowed the conflict to define us for too long. It has overtaken our lives so much that we have been colonized by it" (*Bitter Wormwood*, 236). One needs to adapt history according to the need of time, or if necessary, push it out. One must learn to let go of the past—the past of conflict, if it only increases the 'cycle of vengeance'. They must not allow the history of conflict to continue its influence on present and future.

Neibou was able to do so in case of his grandfather's murder. He could forgive the murder itself, if not the murderers. If he had followed their 'old culture' of taking revenge, it would have destroyed him and nothing good could come of it (*Bitter Wormwood*, 241-42). Instead of clinging to the past, Neibou chooses 'to survive', to come out of the past.

Once exasperated, Mose's friend Neitou had said, "...If a complete stranger came here, an outsider, and asked, 'What is the problem with you Nagas? What do you really want?' I would say to him, 'All we want is peace... First, we were fighting Indian Occupation from 1947.... Then...factionalism made Nagas kill their fellow Nagas. Then the Indian government... impose[d] Indian citizenship on us.... Naga children are being taught they are Indians but when they go to the Indian cities they are completely alienated by the Indian population'" (*Bitter Wormwood*, 212). So, apart from the effort on their part, they also need to be accepted and included into the mainstream population of India.

In the Indian context, socially achieved inclusive nationalism basically implies inclusion of backward section of people, as supported by Gandhi. But during the partition of 1947, several Princely states who sought their independence were incorporated either in India or Pakistan. The people of states like Nagaland found themselves dislocated due to non-identification with the wider Indian culture. There is a need to include these dislocated people into the mainstream India through inclusive nationalism, with the condition that their distinctive identity is not lost in the process.

The first step towards it would be to remove racism. Neibou goes to Delhi for higher studies and encounters maltreatment from others which makes him question his identity as an Indian: "I know that. I am Indian on paper because when I fill up a form and they ask for my nationality, I have to write Indian. But... racism...makes me feel very hopeless about the rights we have been promised by the Indian constitution. Becoming a state in India didn't really change anything much" (*Bitter Wormwood*, 208). Thus, the Nagas are politically Indian but not socially.

A socially achieved inclusive nationalism brings Tagore's idea of India. He imagined a civilization embedded in the tolerance encoded in various traditional ways of life in a highly diverse society, welcoming all peoples and cultures: "Races ethnologically different have come in this country in close contact.... It is our mission to face it and prove our humanity in dealing with it...in India, our difficulties being internal, our history has been the history of social adjustment" (Tagore, *Nationalism*, 14-15). Overcoming social, racial and cultural differences is integral to a positively progressive nationalism.

II

The contention claiming for inclusive nationalism over ethno-cultural conception of nationality is finely established by Arupa Patangia Kalita in her fearless work, *The Story of Felanee* (2011). The novel challenges the classical concept of essentialism, which bounds human beings to claim their identity as characterized by a particular set of attributes to become a fixed entity, and simultaneously re-establishes the holistic and humanist conception of identity. The novel is situated in the 1960s, 70s and 80s conflict ridden times of Assam. And it was during this period that people of Assam were wildly swept by the essence of nationalism, that was particularly ethnic and cultural in nature. This spirit of Assamese nationalism though united the people of Assam, but only in parts. They identified their own independent community and portrayed "the 'other' or the 'non-self' as the 'non-human', undeserving of human feeling", and therefore directed justified violence against them (Abhijit Ghosh, 164). But amidst such violence and conflict, there is a yearning for a resolution or a final solution that could only be achieved through inclusiveness. Therefore, there is a positive inclination towards inclusive nationalism; and mainly towards socially achieved inclusive nationalism that distinctively overcomes internal social barriers for peaceful human existence. This spirit of inclusiveness is portrayed in the novel through the character of Felanee. The narrative demonstrates the need for socially achieved inclusive nationalism through two perspectives. First, it implicitly identifies the need for inclusiveness by challenging the essence of ethno-nationalism. That is, it deconstructs the celebrated notion of ethnic and communal identity and proves it to be a conflicted and unresolved issue, and consequently compels to shift towards inclusiveness. Secondly, the novel directly calls for inclusive nationalism on social and humanitarian grounds. There is always an echo for inclusive human identity sounding at the backdrop of conflict, bloodshed and violence.

Arupa Patangia Kalita's novel sketches the story of "Felanee—the throw away", beginning from her past ancestry, her tragic birth during the 1960's Language Movement of Assam, the killing of her husband and others in a massacre during the 1970's and 80's Assam Movement, to her penurious condition in rehabilitation camp and then in a wretched settlement near a Rabha village.

In the novel, Felanee stands out as a symbol of hybrid subjectivity. Though she survives as an orphan, her ethnic descent clutches her to belong to a community—whether it is her grandmother Ratnamala's Assamese community, her grandfather Kinaram Boro's community, her father Khitish

Ghosh's Bengali community or her husband Lambodar Koch's community. She cannot identify herself with any one ethnic community and therefore could not comprehend her situation when asked to either take off the gold rimmed shell bangles or wear a dokhona.

Biren Baishya looked at Felanee and shouted angrily, "Didn't I tell you to take off those bangles? I told you that they would be your undoing. You belong to a Koch family, yet here you are, with these Bengalis! Take off those wretched bangles at once, I tell you!" (*The Story of Felanee*, 32).

> ...It was a green and red dokhona with a yellow flowered border. In prickly tone, he said, "If you want to survive, wear this." (*The Story of Felanee,* 178)

Instead of submitting to her situation and accepting the imposed identity, what is more important is her own reflection and choice that deconstructs the fundamental basis of ethno-nationalism. It is, therefore, seen that she does not take off those bangles as they "held her mother's fragrance", and she even refuses to wear the dokhona (Bodo traditional dress) which Bulen brings to her for her safety.

Ethno-nationalism is necessarily about ethnic exclusiveness where the subjects show their loyalty to a particular ethnic or racial group rather than to a nation. It is believed that due to their common ethnic or racial origin, members of a particular community have the same ancestors and can be regarded as "relatives". This sentiment of ethno-nationalists stimulated them to preserve and extend the particular ethnic group's identifying characteristics. And therefore, one such way to show ethno-nationalism was to use the ethnic "mother tongue" rather than the official national language. Hence, with this spirit of ethno-nationalism, the language riots started in Assam.

The text portrays many instances of those period of riots and movement in Assam which shows the hatred and inhumane treatment towards people, propagated by the exaggerated ethno-nationalist spirit. One such instance of hatred could be witnessed when "two senior leaders" leading the ethnic cleansing "told the Assamese people to forget words like humanity, love and compassion. They must learn to be hard" (*The Story of Felanee,* 20). This dehumanizing attitude of ethno-nationalists can further be seen in the episode at the rehabilitation camp where the pregnant, sick and traumatized Felanee was kept untreated by the doctors for suspecting her to be a Bengali and therefore a 'a non-human' and 'outsider'. There are also instances of massacre which gave them nothing but blood, fire, brutal killings and death. The description of the aftermath of massacres left one with horrified and desolate scenes:

> ...Felanee walked ahead with the other people. All that met her eyes were half-burnt houses and granaries that had turned into heaps of ashes.... She noticed that the people around her were holding their noses to ward off a foul smell (of dead bodies). Felanee looked up at the tree and emitted a piercing scream. Dangling from the branches of the tree were chopped hands and feet, and two babies without heads. (*The Story of Felanee,* 36)

The novel throughout its narrative deconstructs the spirit of ethno-nationalism but, it also goes a step further in re-establishing the liberal humanist conception of the individual human essence, which ultimately shows the text's inclination towards inclusive nationalism. Here, Felanee acts as a strong force in putting humanness above everything and shows her unconscious urge for inclusiveness:

> Another boy in a white coat, examined her, and remarked that the baby's condition was not good. He then asked her, "What are you, anyway?" Stunned at this question, she kept looking at him...muttered the question to herself "What are you?" Yes, she thought, what am I? "Just a human being, what else?" she said. Biren Baishya and the boy just heard that one word: "human". (*The Story of Felanee*, 32)

Felanee's resistance to an ethnic Assamese identity being imposed on her, shows her unwillingness to surrender her subjectivity and rather wants to resolve the question of her ethnic identity. Here, she feels a need for an all-inclusive world where she could live freely without claiming her ethnic identity. This world of inclusiveness was built up in a new settlement where most of the inmates of the refugee camps along with Felanee and her resided in the latter part of the story. Though the residents of the settlement belonged to different communities, whether it is Kali Boori, Jon's mother, Minoti, Ratna's mother or Felanee, ethnicity never became important enough to affect interpersonal relationships and their lives, and incidents of violence are external disruptive forces. This settlement where the so-called "locusts" of the Assamese society reside, is a perfect symbol of inclusiveness. The residents just require a way to improve their condition—they just want to earn for survival, and nothing else matters. So, throughout the novel Kalita has shown the sensibility and conscious desire of a common man, that is nothing but peaceful existence which is only possible through the spirit of inclusive nationalism.

Conclusion

Inclusive nationalism is necessary to reconcile nation and diversity. Inclusive nationalism avoids fixed identities and embraces shared set of ideals, goals and aspirations. Ethno-nationalism, on the other hand, is characterised by racism, a fear of loss of identity and often a fear of foreigners. It can be said that inclusive nationalism is more liberal, while ethno-nationalism is narrow in nature. Countries like India need inclusive form of nationalism that can avoid separatist forms of nationalism.

References

Ghosh, Abhijit. "Making the Genes in the Blood: Exploring the problematics of Ethnic Identity in *The Story of Felanee*", *Postcolonial Interventions*, Vol. II, Issue 1.

Kalita, Arupa Patangia. *The Story of Felanee*. Translated from Assamese by Deepika Phukan. New Delhi: Zubaan, 2011.

Kire, Easterine. *Bitter Wormwood*. New Delhi: Zubaan, 2011.

Sanyu, Visier Meyasetsu. *A Naga Odyssey*. New Delhi: Speaking Tiger Publishing Pvt. Ltd., 2018.

Tagore, Rabindranath. *Nationalism*. Norwood, USA: J.S. Cushing Co.-Berwick & Smith Co., Norwood Press, 1917.

Kerr, Kathleen. "Race, nation, and ethnicity", *Literary Theory and Criticism*. Edited by Patricia Waugh, New Delhi: OUP, 2016.

7

Nationalism and Social Realism in Tabish Khair's *Filming: A Love Story*

Arun Nath

Introduction to the Social Realism and Nationalism Theory

Social Realism is a literary movement that begins in France with the writings of Gustave Flaubert (1821-1880) and Honore de Balzac (1799-1850). It was sustained in England through the novels of George Eliot (1819-1880), and was introduced in the United States of America by the writings of William Dean Howell (1837-1920). All these novelists wherever they belong to, despite their different cultural background they are interested in the depiction of the influences of the social class and ethnicity on urban life in America. The authors of this period are deploying the method of the Social Realism that is kaleidoscopic in nature and it has been constituted by the various groups, economic classes and ethnic societies. The Movement of Social Realism is influenced by Russian Revolution, Soviet Communism, and International Marxism. These Social Movements concentrates on the welfare of the society and fight for the rights of common people. It becomes very popular all over the world. Thus, the Social Realism in literature spreads worldwide in accordance with the need of the contemporary period. The basic tenets of Social Realism theory are: Racism, Class Struggle, Immigration, Cultural Issues, Humanism, Economic condition of downtrodden class, Ethnicity, Identity Crisis and Social Anxiety which chiefly focus on some social welfare and human issues.

Nation, as one of such collectivities, has almost become fundamental to the existence of human beings in different socio-political situations. Individuals, in one way or other, participate in the concept of nation. Individuals, no doubt, decide the nuances of nation but simultaneously are affected by the constant negotiating stance of a nation. The concept of nation creates a simultaneous situation of inclusion and exclusion: inclusion of its constituent elements as its part and exclusion of the members who are connected with other similar groupings. Individuals feel connected with their nation and consequently find themselves distanced from other nations. However, the simplicity about the concept of nation is deceptive and there are many issues which come forward while unraveling of its abstractness and complexity. Defining a nation involves the evolutionary facts, the temporal and spatial contexts, the ideological parameters, the social standing of individuals, the intricacy of sociopolitical situations, the economic imbroglio, and the identity based cultural tangles.

The concept is variously referred to and analyzed through connected terms, namely, 'nation'; 'nation-state'; 'national'; 'nationalism'; 'nationhood'; and 'nationality' and again with a disagreement on the meanings and connotations of these related terms. Moreover, the concept of nation is directly associated with different fields of Political Science, Sociology, Anthropology, History, Cultural Studies, Linguistics, and Postcolonial Studies and indirectly with many other disciplines and its multidisciplinary nature adds to its profundity and complexity. The present form of the concept of nation is comparatively a new development in the history of human thought. The *Oxford Advanced Learner's Dictionary* defines nation as—"a country considered as a group of people with the same language, culture and history, who live in a particular area under one government" or 'all the people in a country.' The *New Webster Dictionary* refers to 'nation' variously as, "a people inhabiting a certain territory and united by common political institutions; the country or the territory itself; an aggregation of persons speaking the same or a cognate language and use sharing a common ethnic origin".

Objectives

1. To study the Social Realism theory.
2. To study the Nationalism Theory.
3. To implement the basic tenets of Social Realism and Nationalism Theory in Tabish Khair's *Filming: A Love Story.*
4. Methodology: This study is both descriptive and analytical and the data is collected from both the primary and secondary sources. The secondary sources include books, articles, journals and internet sources.

Social Realism in the East

Indian fiction in English witnessed a spurt in Social Realist in the 1980s and 1990s. This Movement came to an end in European fiction at the close of the 19th century, but in the Indian scenario, we witness its rebirth in the fiction of Mulk Raj Anand, R.K. Narayan, Raja Rao and many other stalwarts. The nascent Indian society has been suffering from many social injustice and the creative mind of the novelists reacted sympathetically to the woes of the downtrodden and the marginalized. In the fictional works our new generation writers like—Vikram Seth, Manju Kapur, Aravind Adiga, Arundhati Roy and Tabish Khair, Social Realism has a comeback with an added vigour and vitality. Manju Kapur, Aravind Adiga and Tabish Khair handle realism with its classical characteristics and their writings are like a mirror held against the uncomfortable realities of Indian society. The impact of far-reaching on the Indian social and political Scene called by Gandhian Movement can be perceived in K.S. Venkataramani's *Murugan, The Tiller* (1927) and *Kandan, The Patriot: A Novel of New India in the Making* (1932). Then came A.S.P. Ayyer, whose novels are like *Baladitya* (1930) and *Three Man Destiny* (1939), although untouched by the twentieth century models and set in ancient Indian history, are Gandhian in spirit. The novelists and their novels paved the way for great trinity: Mulk Raj Anand, R.K. Narayan and Raja Rao whose emergence was the most remarkable event in the realm of Indian English fiction. They are the harbingers of the true

Indian English novel. These novelists began writing around the mid-1930s. Bhabani Bhatacharya was also a contemporary of these novelists by birth, but he started writing fiction just after the Indian Independence. Mulk Raj Anand (1905-2004) has been the more prolific of the trio. His contribution to Indian English fiction of Social Realism controvertibly great. His novels including *Untouchable* (1935), *Coolie* (1936), *Two Leaves and a Bud* (1937) portray vividly the wretched of Indian rural society, solves their problems and guide them. The convention of Social Realism in Indian English fiction, established by Mulk Raj Anand, went flourishing during the nineteen fifties and early sixties through Bhabani Bhatacharya, Monohar Malgonkar and Khushwant Singh. Social Realism was also adopted by Hindi Films of the 1940s and 1950s, Chetan Anand's *Neecha Nagar* (1946) which won the Palme d'Or at the first Cannes Film Festival, and Bimal Roy's *Two Acres of Land* (1953), which won the International Prize at the 1954 Cannes Film Festival. The success gave rise to the Indian New Wave, with early Bengali Art Films such as Ritwik Ghatak's *Nagarik* (1953) and Satyajit Ray's *The Apu Trilogy* (1955-59), Social Realism in Indian cinema dates back to the 1920s and 1930s with early examples including V. Shantaram's films *Indian Shylock* (1925) and *The Unexpected* (1937).

Social Realism in the West

In the beginning of 19th century, the industrial revolution and the rise of middle-class society have stung the interest in the depiction of the social realism in literature. The literature has shifted its focus from the elite people to the everyday working-class life. The novels written in this period depict the life of the protagonist which can be identified with the common man of the contemporary period. The thematic issues of this literature were not the romantic or adventurous one or the setting was not the utopian landscapes but on the contrary it was ordinary scene from the neighbourhood. The characters neither belong to the aristocratic society nor they confront with any heroic, unbelievable deeds but they were simply common men of the society, who are suppressed by the over burden of the power politics, economic crises and dynamics of culture. Before the rise of realism, literature was judgmental in approach as the authors of this tradition attempts to criticize the social scene and points out that what is wrong and what is write. This approach restricts them from the selection of the kaleidoscopic thematic aspects or the exploration of social scenes in their full colours.

This brief survey of the tradition of American Realism will enable us to draw the features of the Realism in the American context. The authors of this period deployed the method of social realism to portray the picture of various social groups, economic classes and ethnic societies. The authors of this tradition are—Henry James, Booker T. Washington, Abraham Cahan, Edith Wharton, Edith Maud Eaton, W.E.B. Du Bois, Theodore Dreiser, and Anzia Yezierska. It cannot be claimed that the realism was a monopoly of a specific country or it is restricted in a particular century. All these above-mentioned authors, wherever they belong to, despite of their different cultural background they are interested in the depiction of the influence of the social class and ethnicity of urban life in America. In their literature they use the commonplaces as their setting and the everyday event as their action. The dramatic twists were created with the help of the social problems faced by their characters.

Henry James (1843-1916) is one of the well-known authors of America who contributes a lot to the literature of Social realism. He writes not only the realistic novels but also prepares a critical background for the realism by his non-fictional writings. His fictional works create a realistic social scene and authenticated it with the description of the human psyche. Booker T. Washington (1856-1915) is an African-American author, his autobiographies and critical essays focus on the lives of black immigrants in America. The oppression of black slaves and their social status was the major subject matter of his writing and speeches. He is a well-known social activist and a reformer in American social history. Abraham Cahan (1860-1951) contributes to the literature of realism in America with his debuted novel *Yekl: A Tale of the New York Ghetto* (1896). It is a story of the graphic representation of cultural integration of Russo-Jewish immigrant. Theodore Dreiser (1871-1945) an American author who was considered as a member of Naturalism School. His novels depict the socio-economic life of America. Edith Wharton (1862-1937), with her elite heritage, wrote several novels and short stories while depicting realistic, psycho-logically nuanced portraits of people representing the urban high society. She uses the dramatic irony to emphasise the reality of her contemporary period. Her novels *The House of Mirth* (1905) and *The Age of Innocence* (1920) are significant contribution to the American literature in which she criticises several aspects of his society. In fact, this period can be seen as the transition period in the literary history of America as many authors still linger into the romantic period of literature. Anzia Yezierska (1880-1970), another influential woman author of America, depicts the immigrant life of Jewish community at Manhattan. The issues depicted in her works are primarily the issues of the contemporary women. The social, economic and political status of women is the major subject that centres round her novels. Her works reflect her real-life experiences and therefore counted under the title of realism. These two examples are sufficient to point out that how these authors, as they belong to different ethnic origin, depict the various problems of the society. The real picture of the elite high-class society can be observed in the writings of Wharton whereas the real picture of the immigrants can be seen in the short stories of Yezierska. Therefore, it has been revealed that these authors are using the narrative style and depicting the thematic issues of the literary movement of Social Realism. Their literary works have been written in such a manner that they reflect faithfully an actual way of life.

In the traditional prose narratives, authors always try to create an idealistic world in which every social evil and the voices of the characters are replaced by the idealistic social space and attribute their characters with the heroic qualities. In the literary realism, the focus always lies on the objective description of the society as it is without asserting any romantic feature. So, the authors deal with what is there instead of what should be there. In this connection, it will be worthwhile to understand the opinions of Raymond Williams which he has discussed in his famous essay, "Realism and the Contemporary Novel". He defines the term realism as:

> To put it in more general terms, I mean this. There is a kind of novel which in fact creates and judges the quality of a whole way of living in terms of the qualities of persons.... The distinction of this tradition is that it offers a valuing creation of a whole way of life, a society, that is larger than any of the individuals composing it, and at the same time valuing creations of individual human beings, who while belonging to and affected by and helping to define this way of life, are also, in their own terms, absolute ends in themselves. Neither element, neither the society nor the individual, is there as a priority. The society is not a background against which the personal relationships are studied, nor are the individuals merely illustrations of aspects of the way of life. I call this the realistic tradition because it seems to me to represent a particular kind of mature realism in experience. This, I am saying, is how life is, how I see it when I am trying to see it whole. Every aspect of personal life is radically affected by the quality of the general life, and yet the general life is seen at its most important in completely personal terms. We have to attend with our whole senses to every aspect of the general life, yet the centre of value is always in the individual human person—not any one isolated person, but the many persons who are the reality of the general life. Tolstoy and George Eliot, in particular, often said, in much these terms, that it was this view of life they were trying to realize. (1958: 22)

Williams focuses how the society plays a significant role in the life of an individual and therefore suggests that in a realistic narration the priority is neither society nor an individual. Further he sustains the argument that realism means not just: "...detailed stocking descriptions of shops or back-parlor or station waiting-rooms" (1958: 22). The realistic novels can use it as setting of their action but the realistic description of these settings means not the essence of realism. Further in the essay he made a distinction between the social novel and personal novel. According to him in the social novel the focus of an author is on the accurate observation and description of the general life whereas in the personal novel the author accurately observes and describes persons. This comparison clearly points out "each lacks a dimension, for the way of life is neither aggregation nor unit, but a whole invisible process" (1958: 22). Further he proposes a valid set of characteristic features of a 'realist work'. Williams argues that there are four criteria under which a realist narrative can be evaluated and they are common to all the forms of realism. According to him the first characteristic feature of a realist text is that it should be secular. It means that man should not be judged with the established superstitions and mysticism which surrounds him in the context of society and culture. This separation of man from the superstitions he propelled towards reason and logic. Therefore, according to him realis writing prefers to illustrate the human truth instead of divine truths. The second criterion of realistic novel according to him is that such novels should be grounded in the contemporary scenes in the terms of characters, setting and social issues. In third criterion he suggests that realist narrative should be the social extension. According to this criteria realist text tends to extend the range of characters and topics to include marginal or suppressed groups of the society. The fourth criteria of the realist text is the intention of the author (1958: 50). These criteria are useful to understand the development of Realism from nineteenth century to the twentieth century.

Major Exponents of Social Realism Theory

Major exponents of social realism theory are—Ben Shahn, David Alfaro Siqueiros, Dorothea Lange, Grant Wood, Walker Evans, Raphael Soyer, Thomas Hart Benton, Diego Rivera, Jose Clemente Orosco, Antonio Berni, Jacob Lawrence, Herry Sternberg, William Gropper, Gustave Leonard de Jonghe, Russel Lee, Arther Rothstein, Aron Siskind, Horace Pippin, Walt Kuhn and others.

Tabish Khair was born in Ranchi and grew up in Gaya, a small Indian town of historical interest in Bihar, in a Muslim middle-class family. He pursued a B.A. in History, Sociology and English at Gaya College and a Masters' in English from Magadh University. Khair's early commitment with social and political issues and with writing led him to work as the district reporter for the Patna Edition of *The Times of India*. After troubles with fundamentalists, he moved to Delhi, where he became a staff reporter for the same prestigious newspaper. Four years afterwards, at the age of thirty, Khair moved to Copenhagen, Denmark to undertake his Ph.D. while he earned his living by dishwashing, floor cleaning and the other labour forced upon immigrants. When he finished his study in 2000, there were no academic opportunities there, so he moved to Aarhus, where he is currently an Associate Professor in the Department of English at the University of Aarhus.

Tabish Khair's novel *Filming: A Love Story* (2007), is set in India and spanning the 20th century. The novel deals with social and historical events including assassination of Mahatma Gandhi, the rise of photography and the Bombay film industry and the development of barbed wire with everyday moment that make up the main fabric of our life. The novel deals with social maladies. It tells a series, including that of one-time prostitution, Durga who is persuaded to give away her young son, Ashok, and that of Saleem, the son of a prostitute and two-times star of the silver screen. It is a socio-cultural narrative.

Harihar is a man whose heart is so firmly wedded to his dreams that he has little love remaining for flesh-and-blood reality. He quits his job as a postal clerk in 1920s India and pursues his obsession with film-making with the single-minded intensity of Ahab questing for a white whale. He meets a prostitute 15 years his junior, who does not sleep with him but listens to his dreams, and they end up marrying. But Harihar is a Hindu and the prostitute must change her Muslim name to Durga, one of *Filming's* many instances of attempts to sidestep reality. Its plot, like a Bollywood melodrama, teems with characters and incident, unspooling from their meeting to the present day. Dream sequences are intertwined with potted histories of two inventions, barbed wire and photography, as

Khair is fascinated by them as ways of defining a borderless reality—a central theme in a novel with Partition as its backdrop.

Loneliness and longing permeate Filming, for we are always alone in dreams. The couple initially travel together through the country with their son Ashok, showing silent films to rural audiences, but there is an unbridgeable emotional gulf between them as Harihar ignores Durga's pining for roots and stability. Then Harihar sells Ashok to a landowner's son in exchange for becoming a film director in a studio near Bombay, a "house of ghosts" rather than a longed—for real home to Durga, who works there too. This allows Khair to depict the infant movie industry of the 1940s, and also show celluloid dreams and history colliding; violence comes to the studio as the previously harmonious relationship between Hindus and Muslims becomes tense in the aftermath of Indian independence and the birth of Pakistan.

Often unable to inhabit the present moment, the characters of the novel tend to slide instead between traumatic memories and grandiose dreams, and it is here that the novel finds its considerable emotional force. They are drawn back to moments that they can neither forget nor forgive, entangled in the barbed wire of history, attached to the past by pain is compelled to remember a whipping from his father and the humiliation of his mother watching him being beaten with birch sticks but failing to rescue him.

Khair's narrative method and style erase boundaries, bringing together the normally separate. Words roll into each other without punctuation in the dream sequences, which return to the disastrous fires of 1947 and different times coexist in each character's mind, a magical darkness that recurring metaphors compare to a movie theatre. It's a technique that is sometimes trying and even exhausting, but it can also be highly effective. The novel does something rather different. It is more like a mystery story, in which the reader is taken on an intellectual journey along with a Berlin-based Indian student who is trying to research the life of a Muslim scriptwriter named Batin. As the novel progresses, we are able to see through layers of deception and misperception to an inkling of the truth about Batin and the events of a certain day in 1948, shortly after Indian independence and the partition.

The novel is structured in seven parts or reels with a brief intermission between the third and fourth part. Each of these reels begins with a short chapter named after one of Bharatamuni's eight dramatic Sentiments, or Rasas: there is Rasa Terrible, Rasa Heroic, Rasa Erotic, Rasa Marvellous, Rasa Pathetic, Rasa Furious and Rasa Idious. Rasa Comic is absent: this young man takes himself very seriously. The subject of these chapters is dreaming, and the dreams are presented in breathless, unpunctuated prose, carrying the reader forward. The dreams take place as he sleeps outdoors during a week in January 1948. We gradually come to realise who he is and why he is sleeping outside in a village far from his home city during these winter days, and other parts of the narrative allow us to realise how he has been manipulated by cynical political forces which exploit his Hindu nationalism and idealism. At first the dreams are narrated in the first person, but as soon as he wakes he becomes the man with the binoculars in the third person. Rasa Furious, however, at the beginning of Part VI, frames his dream within a memory from later years: "In later years he would remember this as the last dream, a strangely prescient nightmare"—a dream of killing Mahatma Gandhi, two days before Gandhi's actual assassination. The last part opens with Rasa Odious, not a dream but a reflection from later times. 'Hé Ram' Was that the elusive phrase of his dreams, he wondered in later years. The phrase 'Hé Ram' ('Oh God'), believed to be Gandhi's last words, is inscribed on his memorial in New Delhi.

That this self-important young man, so proud of having been chosen to lead the siege of the Rajkunwar Studios in the village of Dallam, which he believes are "festering with Muslims, communists, traitors, immoral men and women, so that even the light from the chinks in its windows seems to him to be viscous and yellow, oozing like pus, is presented primarily to us as he is being buffeted by dreams—often violent, sometimes erotic—perhaps indicates his general powerless. He is clearly on the side of the forces which are threatening the lives of the other characters in the novel—the main characters—but we gradually realise intellectually what has been implied by this presentation: that he is as much at the mercy of forces beyond his control and comprehension as are the characters in the studio, whom we have come to sympathise and, perhaps, identify with.

After the first of these dreams, 'Reel-I' continues with a seemingly straightforward narrative, so traditional that it begins. But after a few pages this story of the arrival of the bioscope-wallah and his wife and child at a haweli outside the village of Anjangarh is interrupted by a passage in italics, enclosed in quotation marks, about Seth Dharamchand's business interests in film and barbed wire, which seems to have little bearing on the story currently being narrated. The speaker realises this and apologises:

> If I remember correctly, young man, Seth Dharamchand had an unofficial monopoly on all government contracts, before and after Independence. But I haven't told you about the Seth yet, have I? I am sorry, I forgot: we are still almost two decades from Independence. (2007: 11)

In this way, what has seemed like a neutral third-person point of view is revealed to be a story told by someone, years later, to a young man. After a few more pages, there is a passage in bold italics, which is clearly an interpolation into Batin's own narrative by the young scholar, explaining how he came to be interviewing Batin—more because of his availability than from any significance he thought him to have. This pattern continues throughout the novel, and as we come to realise toward the end, the bulk of the narrative is in fact told by Batin, and the reason he knows so much about all these people—the Chotte Thakur/Rajkunwar, Harihar/Hari Babu, Durga/Bhuvaneshwari and Saleem Lahori (a question which has puzzled the scholar to the point of exasperation) is that he and his wife were both major players in the story he is relating. Batin says to the young man, "stories are impossible to fence in either time or space, and I was told this story by three different people, from three different perspectives" (2007: 71). Only gradually do we, and the young scholar, come to realise that Batin is failing to declare his own place in the story, but doing so in a way which draws attention to the mystery: in fact, he seems to be begging the young man to find him out. His last words to the scholar are, "If you have listened to my account, surely you will be able to fill in the blanks. If you have listened" (2007: 362). This challenge from Batin to the young man is also an indirect challenge from the author to the reader.

But Batin does not have a monopoly on this narrative. Apart from the young Hindu extremist with the colourful dreams, there is a woman doctor in a provincial Indian town, who recounts to the same young scholar a visit to the cinema with her parents some twenty years before, in the early 1970s. We come to realise that this is the daughter of Ashok, the son of Durga and Harihar, and the film they saw at the cinema that night, *Aakhri Raat*, was Harihar's account of the dramatic occurrences in the haweli back in 1929, the film which caused violent arguments between Hari Babu and Rajkunwar at the time of its filming, as recounted by Batin. The woman doctor recollects the discussion between her parents after seeing the film, about his adoption by the Thakur family and what he remembered of his birth parents.

There is an enigmatic Intermission between Reels III and IV: a monologue from Saadat Hassan Manto dated 16 January 1955. Manto, the Urdu writer who left India for Lahore in 1948, died on 18 January 1955 of cirrhosis of the liver. In this monologue he addresses a nameless friend, whom we may deduce is Batin or Saleem Lahori, though this may only become clear on a second reading of the novel. Manto says:

> What a story you could tell, my friend, if you decided to. But I know you have pledged not to do so. It is part of your choice of life: what you write will only be fiction. But the facts of your life, you living ghost, what about the facts of your life that are stranger than any fiction? Will you, the writer and the showman in you be able to resist and take them to the grave? Or will you leave some clues behind, cryptic like those literary quotes with which you could pepper a late-night drinking round in Bombay? (2007: 202)

So we are able to piece together a story which really hangs between two dramatic events: the first in 1929, when Harihar gives Ashok up to the Thakur family in exchange for a partnership with the Chotte Thakur in a film studio, and the second in 1948, when the studio is attacked and burned by Hindu nationalists. There are several perspectives on these events, most of them oblique, 'narrated at a tangent'. Not only are there different people telling the story, with different sets of knowledge about the facts, but for some characters discovering the truth is part of the story. Durga discovers in 1947 exactly what had gone on between Harihar and the Chotte Thakur back in 1929, "the secret—they had not given away Ashok for his own good but sold him for their dreams" (2007: 319). Bhuvaneshwari loses touch with her son, but we hear something about his subsequent life from his daughter's interview with the young film scholar, her knowledge having been obtained by eavesdropping on a conversation between her parents when she was a child. Facts revealed in this indirect way build up a haunting and memorable narrative, more powerful than a simple chronological account told from a neutral point of view could ever be. The reader is actively engaged in constructing the story line, not just passively consuming a plot.

The points of view in *Filming* are not so clearly demarcated as those in *The Bus Stopped* by Tabish Khair. The angles of vision could be said to be four-dimensional, where those in the earlier novel are mainly three dimensional: that is, though in both novels the points of view are quite diverse geographically. In *The Bus Stopped* most of the narrative is related from various rhetorical positions not very distant in time from the main events which took place during the bus trip, while in *Filming* the action of the novel, though centering on the events of January 1948, begins nearly twenty years earlier and takes in points of view some decades later, as the young film scholar talks to Batin in Denmark in 1988, and to the woman doctor in the fictional Indian town of Phansa.

Khair carefully provides readers from other linguistic backgrounds with all the information needed to understand the many unfamiliar words he uses. For example, in *Filming* when he introduces the Chotte Thakur, a western reader assumes that Chotte is his first name. However, later there is a conversation between Ashok and the Chotte Thakur's sister-in-law Maalkini. Ashok knew by now that the children of her extended family called her Badi Ma but had not heard any of the children of servants calling her that and doubted that children from outside her family would dare claim the intimacy of referring to her as their 'elder mother'. He hesitated: *But I have a Ma, he replied, finally. She smiled, patiently, perhaps even sadly. She is your Chotti Ma. From now on we are your Badi Ma* (2007: 116).

Tabish Khair has succeeded quite magnificently with *Filming*, which continues to haunt the echo chambers of the mind long after the last page has been read. The story, refracted as it is through so many points of view, takes on a mythical, enigmatic quality, and the work the reader has to do to reconstruct and interpret the facts encourages the feeling of a shared experience, more valuable than the kind of commodified storytelling fiction he criticises, which is aimed at consumers rather than readers.

Conclusion

To sum up, after implementing the basic tenets of Nationalism and Social Realism theory: Racism, Class Struggle, Immigration, Cultural Issues, Humanism, Ethnicity, Economic condition of downtrodden class, Identity Crisis and Social anxiety in Tabish Khair's *Filming: A Love Story* we are able to map abounds of nationalism and social realism elements. Through a close perusal, it seems that Khair's choice, of his own volition, of a writing career, his struggle with and control over the craft of writing, his struggle for identity in the existing society, and his vibrant and vigorous life are very minutely represented through the character, Batin. So, we can rightly call the novel a nationalism and social realism treatise.

References

Khair, Tabish. *Filming: A Love Story.* London: Picador, 2007. Print.

Bakhtin, Mikhail. "Discourse in the Novel." *Literary Theory: An Anthology*. Ed. Julie Rivkin and Michael Ryan. MA: Blackwell Publishers, 1998. 32-44. Print.

Barry, Peter. *Beginning Theory: An Introduction to Literary and Cultural Theory*. 2nd ed. Manchester: Manchester UP, 2002. Print.

Chandra, N.D.R. "Canon, Multiculturalism & The God of Small Things." *Contemporary Literary Criticism: Theory and Practice*. Delhi: Authorspress, 2005. Print.

Chauhan, Anurag. "Ingenuity and Translation: Meanings of Ghalib in Tabish Khair's 'Man of Glass'". *Journal of Literature, Culture and Media Studies*. Vol. 3, Issue 5. 2011.

Dwivedi, Om Prakash (Ed.). *Tabish Khair: A Critical Companion*. London: Roman Books, 2013. Print.

Farganis, James. *Reading in Social Theory: The Classic Tradition to Post-Modernism*, McGrag Hill Education (India) Edition. 2013. Print.

Gàmez-Fernàndez, Cristina M. & Om Prakash Dwivedi (Eds.). *Tabish Khair: Critical Perspectives*. Newcastle: Cambridge Scholars Publishing, 2014. Print.

Iyengar, K.R. Srinivasa. *Indian Writing in English*. New Delhi: Sterling Publishers, 1962. Print.

Khair, Tabish. *Babu Fictions: Alienation in Contemporary Indian English Novels*. New Delhi: Oxford UP, 2001. Print.

——. "Indian Pulp Fiction in English: A Preliminary Overview from Dutt to Dé." *Journal of Commonwealth Literature* 43.3 (2008): 59-74.

——. "Re-Orientalisms: Meditations on exoticism and transcendence, Otherness and the Self." *Re-Orientalism and South Asian Identity Politics: The oriental Other within*. Ed. Lisa Lau and Ana Cristina Mendes. Routledge Contemporary South Asia Series. 44. New York: Routledge, 2011. 144-58.

Khair, Tabish, Martin Leer & Justin D. Edwards (Eds). *Other Routes: 1500 Years of African and Asian Travel Writing*. Indiana: Indiana UP, 2005. Print.

Loomba, Ania. *Colonialism/Postcolonialism*. 2nd ed. London: Routledge, 2005. Print.

Mellor, Philip. *Religion, Realism and Social Theory: Making Sense of Society.* Thousand Oaks. SAGE Publications Inc., 2004. Print.

Sheela, C. Amutha Charu. "*London Dreams*: Analysis of Tabish Khair's *The Thing About Thugs as an Anti-Colonial Discourse.*" *Language in India* 11(2011). Web. 26 Sep. 2012.

Verma, Renu Kaul, ed. Muslim Modernities: Tabish Khair's *Essays on Moderation and Mayhem* 2001-2007. New Delhi: Vitasta, 2008. Print.

8

Politics of Identity and Home in the Context of Indian Chinese in India: A Study of *Chinatown Days* and *The Palm Leaf Fan*

Doyir Ete

The complex dynamics of home, nation, and nationality most often raises the existential crisis of the most marginal of the minority communities within a Nation-State. India houses several designated minority communities like Muslims, Christians, Parsis, Sikhs and Indian Jews. These communities enjoy rights that the Constitution guarantees to the citizens of the country. But there are also communities who are not designated as minority communities but nevertheless marginalized within the socio-political discourse of the nation because of their precarious position entailed by a checkered history of migration, settlement, and experience in India. The Chinese community settled in India is an exemplary of such a group whose history presents an intriguing insight into a journey that is rich yet turbulent, joyous yet heart wrenching at the same time. It becomes imperative to interrogate and present an overview of the writings and the social context of stories narrating the complex journey of the Chinese community settled in India. Every minority community like the Parsis and Indian Jews have their own history of migration and settlement in India. Like them the Chinese Indians also has a history that narrates their arrival during the colonial period and subsequent settlement predominantly in Calcutta and Makum in Assam. The Chinese Indian experience in India has been very less documented and there are very few firsthand accounts of their life in India. A well-known work is Sahitya Akademi Awardee, Rita Chowdhury's *Chinatown Days* (2018) which narrates the history and trials of the Chinese Assamese community settled in Makum, and their trauma during the Sino-Indian dispute of 1962. Kwai-Yun Li's *The Palm Leaf Fan and Other Stories* (2006) is based on the Chinese Indian experience in Calcutta and the stories are a product of her experience of growing up in Calcutta with the Chinese and Indians jostling for space in her narratives. It is pertinent to point out the many similarities in the shared experience of the Chinese Indians in the two books points to the fact that the central crux of the Chinese experience in India was the Indo-China war of 1962 and its cataclysmic effect on the psychology as well as the socio-cultural fabric of the community both, in Calcutta and Makum. What also cannot be missed is the location from which the two authors have explored the presence of the Chinese Indians in India and the critical engagements that have taken the readers into this otherwise unexplored part of Indian society and culture. Rita Chowdhury is a known and established writer from Assam. A passionate artist she is very vocal about her commitment to narrating the many untold stories about human suffering, endurance, marginal voices, and history. Her activism during her student days, particularly her journey as a political prisoner during the agitation of Assam movement has made her sensitive to littlest of events that contains big stories. I have been fortunate to listen to her at the Arunachal Literary Festival in the year 2019 at Itanagar and again honoured to share stage with her along with acclaimed authors Dhruba Hazarika and Sahitya Akademi Awardee Rashmy Narzary at the North East Book Festival at Guwahati in the year 2019. At both the meetings, Rita Chowdhury appealed to my keen readership with her delicate sensibilities, her choice of subjects, and her love for writing. *Chinatown Days* was a product of intense research as well as close personal conversations with people who had lived through that period. Her location as an academician, activist as well as an established author has all gone into creating a novel that is rich in historical facts as well as imaginary details. The novel gives a glimpse into a significant part of Assamese history which began during the colonial era and which is present even today. Surprisingly, even many in Assam came to know of this fascinating part of history only through her novel *Chinatown Days*.

Kwai-Yun Li's location as a Chinese in India gives a firsthand account of the Chinese experience in Calcutta. She was born in Calcutta in 1950 and shifted to Canada in 1972. *The Palm Leaf Fan* a slim collection of different stories is woven together through the persona of the writer. It is through the first-person narrative, we traverse through intimate and personal accounts of different Chinese characters living in an Indian milieu in different parts of Calcutta. In this case too, the collection can also be read as a documentation of the history of the Chinese people who have already been living in the country for many years. According to Kwai-Yun Li, the First Chinese ship to arrive in Calcutta was in the 1770s under the ownership of a merchant named Yang Da Zhao, also referred to as Acchi who was the owner of the ship. According to a popular Chinese legend in Calcutta he tricked Warren Hastings, the Governor General into giving him a large tract of land in and around Calcutta. In another version of the story, Acchi, was sailing through Thailand when he was blown off course and arrived in Calcutta where he traded his ship full of tea with Warren Hastings for a large estate. In Acchi's honor a temple still stands, called Temple of Acchi, in Calcutta. According to this legend the Chinese migration and settlement in Calcutta can be traced to the 18th century and later. Migration happened in different waves according to Kwai-Yun Li. She writes that in 1910s and 1920s more men and women from China arrived bringing the population to around thirty thousand during India's Independence. But, today owing to different reasons; anxiety for their future, statelessness, and marginalization, mass migration has taken place and the numbers have reduced to just three thousand or less Chinese population in Calcutta today.

In *Chinatown Days*, Rita Chowdhury narrates how the Chinese history began in India with the discovery of tea by the British in Assam. She also writes that by 1839 the skilled

Chinese workers had become the East India Company's most valuable assets because of their knowledge of tea cultivation. An aspect of the Chinese migration to India which has been overlooked is the sea passage between China and Calcutta where scores of Chinese migrants died. The terrible stories of abduction, starvation, sickness, and death as they were huddled into ships reminds the passage across the Atlantic, as ships ferried Africans to their destiny of slavery in Europe and America. For the Chinese who came to Assam a journey further from Howrah, and then upstream on Brahmaputra awaited them; it took three months to reach Assam. Broken and tired by the journey and the nightmarish experience at the hands of their handlers, the Chinese found some peace in the interiors of Assam as they began to settle down to a routine life of some kind. They were sent wherever they were needed, to dig trees, planting and plucking tea leaves, building houses and water pumps: there was not a single work in the tea plantation that the Chinese did not attend to. The author writes,

> They feared never seeing their homeland or their loved ones again.... The world they had left behind was slowly passing into obscurity. They did whatever was asked of them without any protest. Their infinite sighs had mixed with the air of the tea gardens of Assam. A million drops of their sweat mixed with the freshly dug soil of the gardens. (Chowdhury 2018, 65-65)

The Chinese Indians also qualifies as a diasporic community because of their immigrant position and outsider status in India. It follows naturally that for a community in such a precarious position as the Chinese Indians, the question of nation, nationality, and nationhood become a critical engagement and awareness. Such awareness is also brought about when politics become a part of the common parlance of the community. In both the novels, it is the Indo-China war of 1962 that became a defining moment for the Chinese in India in terms of the rude realization of their outsider status in India. It forced them to reconsider Makum in Assam and Calcutta as their homeland. They were compelled to re-negotiate their lives and like their ancestors they were also forced to experience the forceful separation from their home and family. The trauma experienced because of this event has to a great extent defined the Chinese experience which can be assuaged by the gravity with which Rita Chowdhury and Kwai-Yun Li describes it in their narratives. In *Toward a Theory of Cultural Trauma*, Jeffrey C. Alexander states

> For Traumas to emerge at the level of the collectivity, social crisis must become cultural crisis. Events are one thing, representations of these events quite another. Trauma is not the result of a group experiencing pain. It is the result of this acute discomfort entering into the core of the collectivity's sense of its own identity. Collective actors "decide" to represent social pain as a fundamental threat to their sense of who they are, where they came from, and where they want to go. (Alexander 2004, 11)

The emphasis is on how social crisis must become cultural crisis for a successful collective representation of trauma. Various questions must be asked, and attempts be made to answer them. What had happened to the Chinese Indians during 1962? What were their pains? What happened to individuals and to the group as a whole? Did only families break or did the group as a whole break? Who or what were the agencies involved? What about the moral responsibility and accountability? How can this trauma be represented to a wider audience? Such attempts at representation of social suffering create a new narrative and assume a symbolic significance of a cultural crisis which deeply affects the collective consciousness of a group. In so far as the discussion of the Chinese Indians are concerned the internment and ghettoization during Indo-China war of 1962 consists an inseparable part of their being and existence and to bring it to a wider audience, it entails the preservation and narration of it in different forms of history and memory.

The considerations of Indo-China political dynamics is intimately connected with the ways in which the Chinese Indians are perceived by the Indians and vice versa. Thus, an important reason for recounting the stories of the Chinese experience in India is also to bring to the public domain, what had happened during 1962, and how the Chinese community in India became a pawn in the political battle between two nations. In *Chinatown Days*, as we read the lives of the men and women of the intermixed Chinese Assamese community of Makum, we have a fair idea of what was at stake. The war had its repercussions even on the level of family and it split the social fabric of the multicultural community. In the novel, a police inspector of the Doom Dooma police station scolds his junior Tileswar Baruah as to why he had also arrested local women and children. The junior replies to him in exasperation "A Chinese man has a local wife. His sons also have local wives. Whom to arrest and whom to leave behind? We have left their local wives" (Chowdhury 2018, 239). Also, the senior himself acknowledges that it was difficult to identify the Chinese because some of them did not even look Chinese. Such state intervention during times of war has time and again made the family as the site of struggle and control. Particularly, the question of identity is further complicated, in such cases where a single family consisted of members with both Chinese and Indian heritage and either of the two. Such complex societal relationships called for sensitive interventions but in Makum police and state mishandling caused disruptions that left deep chasms in the minds and bodies of the victims. *Chinatown Days* narrates such local stories that got lost with the victims as they were forced to scatter to different parts of the world. If we look at the small histories imbibed in the stories, we understand how this unique community that existed in Makum also formed an important part of the social fabric of Assam. The national media during 1962 was engrossed in highlighting the Indo-China war but the tragic stories that unfolded in Makum and Calcutta did not catch the attention or the imagination of the public. Particularly, after post-colonialism and post-modernism, the silence over marginal histories has been questioned, and it becomes important on our part to envisage a future by re-establishing a connection with the past and this can be achieved only through foregrounding of such stories.

Kwai-Yun Li's stories also raises number of pertinent questions. How do the Chinese locate themselves in India? How should a nation/state like India respond to the narratives from these minority communities? How does one respond to the predicament and ambivalence that is inherent in their narratives? In an interview to the 'Guiding Star' Kwai-Yun Li states that *The Palm Leaf Fan* is a book about trying to identify what it was like to be a Chinese in Calcutta. The Chinese community was multifaceted with the community engaged in professions in which their ancestors were skilled and trained since generations. Most probably, the skills were imported from China when their ancestors had first migrated to Calcutta. They formed a vibrant part of the social and cultural fabric of the city through their flourishing culinary business, beauty parlous, tannery and shoe making business. Their colorful festivals like the Chinese New Year and the Dragon Dance were famous for their vivacity. Minority communities most often live in isolated and segregated colonies in proximity with each other. Kwai-Yun Li writes

> They lived in two areas: Those who went into the leather-tanning business settled in Tangra, on the eastern fringe of Calcutta. The Chinese who ran furniture factories, hairdressing salons, restaurants, and shoe shops settled in the Bow Bazaar area in northern Calcutta, where Indians of the middle and lower classes lived. (Yun Li 2006, 107)

Living in such proximity is a common feature among immigrant communities because it gives them a sense of security. Choices in livelihood and vocation for communities in minority are also many a times dictated by its social repercussions. What is discernible among them is that they take up occupations which the dominant group within a nation usually does not take up. This offers least danger of confrontation arising out of issues of infringement into the livelihoods of the dominant groups. Not denying the reality that the Chinese had indigenous skills regarding shoe making and leather crafts, they also ventured into the opportunities that arose because of cultural and religious factors in India. The author writes "The Chinese went into businesses which the Hindus found polluting: leather-tanning, hairdressing, shoe-making, carpentry and restaurant-keeping" (Yun Li 2006, 107). Thus, the Chinese business in these occupations boomed and their products were in much demand by the locals. We can get a testimony of this fact in a report in the newspaper *Asia Times* which states

> In the 1950s and 1960s, Calcutta swore by the Chinese expertise. When they needed attention for their teeth, they chose a Chinese dentist, not an Indian. When shopping for a pair of footwear, they walked into the city's Bentinck Street where tens of Chinese shoe shops lined the pavement. Chinese were the best hair-dressers at a time when this art was not known at all to Indians. They cleaned your suits impeccably. And they sold yummy food in restaurants in the city's plus downtown, Chowringhee and Park Street. (*Asia Times*)

Apart from such delightful contributions to the social milieu of Calcutta, the Chinese also displayed their skills in art, dance and music which they performed during Chinese social gatherings and festivals. In his book *Diaspora Criticism* (2006) Mishra writes "Identity is doubtless a useful socio-political tool for minority groups struggling to express their grievances from a disempowered position in any given polity; the part played by the expressive arts and cultures in this struggle is also not to be underestimated" (Mishra 2006, 57). This is attested by the display of Chinese cuisines, leather shoes, Chinese beauty parlors through the main streets of Chinatown in Calcutta. Of the Chinese festivals the most celebrated was the Dragon dance during the Chinese New Year. Sadly, the Dragon dance also faced extinction due to multiple reasons. During the 1962 incarceration of the Chinese by the Indian Government and the subsequent years, the Chinese population who were struggling for their very existence could no longer celebrate their new year with the same enthusiasm. The dwindling number of their members due to emigration could not suffice for the numbers required for the dragon dance. The situation has totally changed today. Dragon dance is kept alive by the female members of the community. The Chinese in Calcutta have the only all-female dragon dance group in the world. The female of the community has adapted to the changing times by defying gender norms and taking unto themselves the task of preserving their unique cultural ethos. This is also a demonstration of the ways in which minority communities defy the onslaughts of globalization on their traditional way of life.

As India got its Independence the Chinese were not left unaffected by the changes that followed. The most traumatic moment for the community came during the Indo-China conflict of 1962. It was a defining moment in terms of state victimization and forced ghettoization of the Chinese who were left at the mercy of the state. They were hounded and huddled into trains to a makeshift camp in Deoli, Rajasthan. Families lost their livelihood and business, their homes and properties were confiscated by the government and in some cases by the locals. Individual victimization because of their ethnicity was also rampant. *Chinatown Days* and *The Palm Leaf Fan* narrate how the Chinese Indians were looked at with suspicion and reviled because they were Chinese. Kwai-Yun Li narrates that the police would come at any time in the night to arrest Chinese families to deport them to the camps in Deoli. So, women like her mother, would pack for individual members emergency kits with all the essential items so that they would be ready for the worst. There was no knowing because the police would usually come at night. She writes "Every Chinese in Calcutta had a pack" (Yun Li 2006, 58). The resentment against them also spread among the locals. They faced ostracism and were boycotted by some sections of shopkeepers. For example, the local shopkeeper refused to sell them light bulbs when they needed to replace the old one. They were harassed with chants of "China go back" whenever they walked on the streets. Politics of terror and fear played out into the streets too. The fear was so much so that the Chinese boys practiced martial arts in case the Indians attacked them. But women like her mother were more sensible who realized that it was more practical to avoid violence since they were already minuscule in numbers. Their liminal position made them more vulnerable. There was always the danger of retaliation. Therefore, she advised the boys to run when they were attacked instead of fighting back. The fear of persecution also compelled the community to demonstrate that they were loyal citizens of India and did not pose a threat because of their ethnicity. The pressure to be model citizens compelled them to take innovative measures to see that their survival is not threatened, and the community came together at such difficult times. For instance, rallies were held by the Chinese in Calcutta to denounce the Communist government in China. Such incidents also took place in Makum, where the Chinese Assamese brought out processions and rallies condemning China and declaring their love for India. A vexed issue between the two nations was also the annexation of Tibet by the Chinese Government. One of the reasons for the Chinese aggression in India was that they were miffed in India for giving refuge to the Dalai Lama. The Dalai Lama became a political tool for the Chinese in Calcutta. For example, in *The Palm Leaf Fan* the narrator's mother states, "If the Indian police see my name more than once, they will know that we are not communists and we support the Dalai Lama, and the police will not take us and lock us away in some horrible place" (Yun Li 2006, 57). Like many Chinese she also starts wearing beads with Dalai Lama's picture on both her wrists to show her support. Similarly, every Chinese school in Calcutta put up a picture of Mahatma Gandhi in their schools. Even the National Anthem began to be sung along with the Chinese Nationalist Anthem. Through these instances we can clearly see the predicaments faced by the community during times of communal tension. Another instance is the adoption of Hindi in the curriculum of the Chinese schools in Calcutta. The predicament is clearly visible when Miss Au complains

> Mr Ma should get someone else to teach Hindi. I do not remember the Hindi alphabet. Yesterday I got the consonants all mixed up in class. No wonder the students looked confused. I was totally confused myself. At this, Miss Chen comforts her and suggests "Hopefully, we'll drop Hindi from our curriculum when this whole mess is over." (Yun Li 2006, 60)

Thus, the Chinese Indian community is compelled to demonstrate its loyalty to India for its very survival. In hindsight it is also an example of how minority communities dexterously adapt to the changing situations and flow with the current of the majority. In this case when the Indo-China war was over and the situation returned to normal Kwai-Yun Li narrates how the Dalai Lama pictures were all discarded and when Communism became popular in Calcutta they heaved a sigh of relief. The changing political dynamics between India and China constantly affected the Chinese population. The civil war between the Communist Party under Mao Tse Tung and the Nationalist Party under Chiang Kai Shek put them in great dilemma. Today, the Chinese Indians continue to remain stateless though many of them were born and raised in India. Being stateless is one of the most marginal position to be especially in an environment of increasing nationalism and jingoism throughout the world. The Chinese were issued Visa which had to be renewed every three months and it allowed them to stay only in Calcutta. Similarly, in Makum too, the documents of the Chinese had to be constantly renewed though many of them were born in India and their parents had come to the country long before Independence. The visa restricted their movement to Calcutta only and curtailed their freedom to travel. It also greatly limited their scope of expanding their business as well as move to other locations for residence. Kwai-Yun Li writes,

> Mother had emigrated from China in the 1920s with a passport from the Nationalist government. In 1950, the Indian Government recognized the Chinese Communist government as the representative of China. Since the Nationalist government in Taiwan did not exist for the Indian Government, India, issued Stateless Alien Visas for all Chinese Nationalist passports. Mother and I became stateless alien. (Yun Li 2006, 57)

Being stateless has many disadvantages which are not just political but economic too. The most distressing is to be a second-class citizen of any nation. The constitution of the nation grants certain rights and privileges to its citizens. Access to resources, education, dignity, and freedom of religion are all guaranteed by the constitution. Such, access to resources, education etc. are not always granted to non-citizens, they are always next in line. In an article in *Asia Times* titled "Kolkata's Chinese Live in Stateless Sorrow" Gautaman Bhaskaran writes "With virtually no rights, these stateless Chinese lead depressing lives. They are sometimes viewed as spies and police question them even in the middle of the night". Prime Minister Nehru's policy towards China which kept vacillating with the establishment of different governments under the Communist Mao Tse-Tung and the Nationalist Chiang Kai Shek made the Chinese Indian's position rather precarious. Liang Ching Wan a character in *Chinatown Days* says that when he had first come to Calcutta at the age of twenty-five there was a battle going on between Chiang Kai Shek and Mao Tse-Tung. Mao Tse-Tung won the battle and the communists removed Chiang Kai Shek from power and formed a new government with Chow En Lai as the Prime Minister. Nehru's friendship with Chow En Lai popularized the cry "Hindi-Chini Bhai Bhai". But it was also true that Nehru had also formed good friendship with the Koumintang government under Chiang Kai Shek previously. The Chinese in India who had supported the Koumintang government which was also the earlier policy of Nehru were suddenly treated as anti-Indian and anti-China. Nehru made a flip flop once Mao Tse-Tung came to power acknowledged his leadership. The Koumingtang supporters were caught between Indian hostility and Chinese resentment. One of the characters in the novel states "Did you know, just to maintain a good relationship with China, Nehru kicked around the Chinese in India like a football" (Chowdhury 2018, 116). Within the hegemony of a Nation-State the diaspora is always the 'other' placed/positioned against the dominant group from whom it differs culturally or religiously. In her interview to the newspaper 'Guardian Star', Kwai-Yun Li says

> ... Hindu society was very caste oriented, and the Chinese, especially the poor Chinese; you don't know where to put them, so they put them with the Untouchables. So, you have to think that, because it was a caste society and we didn't have a caste, so, you had to be careful. The Brahmins wouldn't want to associate with you because, well, you are dirty, you don't have a caste.

Such differentiation and discrimination are observed by Kwai-Yun Li in her short novel. Customs, beliefs, cultural practice, food habits and even physical features which are adjudged as different, exotic, and strange obstruct complete assimilation of a minority group into the main stream of the nation. For instance, in *The Palm Leaf Fan*, Rosie a Chinese friend of the narrator is heckled by few local men "These are the dirty China from down Lal Bazaar way" (Yun Li 2006, 56). Women also face other forms of stereotyping that objectifies them. They are hurled sexist remarks because of their Asian features which make them stand out from their Indian counterparts. For example, in another incident the narrator writes "A banana peel thrown from a balcony hit Miss Au on the shoulder. Two men standing at the bakery laughed and made obscene gestures with their fingers. "Come, come, pretty China, come play with me" (Yun Li 2006, 56). As we observe here language is also used as a tool, to objectify, as well as denigrate them through such abusive words and typecast them because of their physical features. Ironically, sometimes women from the community themselves stereo type their own female members. The Chinese Indians followed strict inter-marriage, perpetuating traditional standards of beauty for Chinese girls. Kwai-Yun Li portrays hoe the Chinese ladies indulged in the sly activity of picking the perfect brides for their sons. She writes how women were very particular about appearance during matrimony alliance. In *The Palm Leaf Fan*, the narrator's mother points out "I would like my grandchildren to have nice noses. I want them to have bridges between their eyes" (Yun Li 2006, 2). She chooses a young girl from the Wong family and says to their mother "Your daughters have nice, fair skin. Good, good" (Yun Li 2006, 3). In the context of an immigrant community like the Chinese Indians how can we explain such discrimination towards the girls? It is important to understand the reasons behind such behavior which is due to socio-cultural factors as well as pressures from society. Inter-marriage proffers ethnic purity and propagation of the ethnic way of life through off springs. The set standards of beauty are internalized by the community members indirectly making Chinese girls as the preferred bride thereby discouraging inter-ethnic marriages and mix-breeding. From a psychoanalytic perspective the shifting subjectivity of a minority problematizes its location in relation to the multicultural milieu of the Nation-

State. There are complex nuances to their experience which cannot be just explained in terms of otherization, assimilation, acculturation, or hybridity. Different subject positions are created because of different experiences and the identity keeps shifting. For example, though they are constantly 'otherised' by the majority of the nation, from their perspective it is the majority who are the 'others'—the non-Chinese. To essentialize the Chinese way of life they follow strict inter-marriage and live a close-knit, segregated life. Traditionally, women are put in charge of their daughters and are responsible for her physical as well as moral upbringing. In nurturing a son, the father acts as a role model imbibing values and teachings according to established norms. A mother's role is important but mostly to an extent that she chooses a suitable bride for her son. Thus, these are some explanations which can help to understand the role of women in stressing inter-marriage and internalized standards of beauty. It is perceived as a duty not only towards the family but also the group at large. Particularly for traditional communities like the Chinese Indians, family has always been an area where debates around issues of marriage, childcare, sexuality, etc. frequently happen; it is a site of control as well as comfort. The dynamics of this space and its power over the members is interesting to examine when engaging with a minority group like the Chinese Indians.

In Makum, the existential crisis for the Chinese Indian community intensified as the discourse of nation and nationalism began to gain ground in the aftermath of the Indo-China war. In *Chinatown Days*, father of Hong and Ming puts this into perspective when he observes in detention "We are Chinese. That is the reality. Even if we live here for a thousand years, this will be our identity. They will not consider us one of them" (Chowdhury 2018, 231). Homi Bhaba in his preface to *The Location of Culture* writes,

> Globalization, I want to suggest, must always begin at home. A Just measure of global progress requires that we first evaluate how globalizing nations deal with 'the difference within'—the problem of diversity

> and redistribution at the local level, and the rights and representations of minorities in the regional domain. (Bhabha 1994, xv)

Today especially when the minorities and their position within the nation has become a raging debate, how can we try to explain the presence of the Chinese Indians and to what extend can we claim to speak on their behalf? These are important but difficult questions. In Makum there was more than an outsider/insider conflict. The circumstances in Makum was unique; the fraternity of Chinese and locals was based on intricate ties not just the tension between foreigners and locals. Makum housed not just Chinese families, but families that had becomes so interlinked and intertwined with the local Assamese that, in fact it comprised of Chinese-Assamese-Indians in a single family! The tea garden migrants from Bihar, Orissa and other parts brought by the British for tea plantation had also mixed with the population thus presenting a truly inter-mixed social unit. So, the forced separation of families during the 1962 war devastated not just the Chinese, but even Assamese and other members. They were not given a chance to political, legal, and social rights. The uncertainty of the Chinese Indian families in Makum is an example of how war between nations tore families apart and broke a peaceful multicultural society. In *Chinatown Days*, Ananta a local boy is in love with Ahlin a Chinese girl. When Indo-China war broke out and emotions were running high, Ananta suddenly felt jittery and unsure about Ahlin. He felt that he was being judged by his friends and especially his loyalty towards India was questioned so much so that he breaks her heart. Mei Lin, a Chinese girl who is married to a local boy Pulok Baruah is betrayed by her father-in-law, dragged from home, crammed into the train along with hundreds of Chinese Assamese to Deoli in Rajasthan. Unknown to Pulok, she is shipped off to communist China. In another case, Phulmoni refuses to go to China with her husband Akong. She wanted to stay back with her children at Makum, but if she did so, Akong would have to part from his children forever. The dilemma was also faced in Tung Chin's house with Xonpahi. She wanted to go with her husband to China but her family refused to send her.

Such anxieties and dilemmas were felt at many different levels. *Chinatown Days* is the story of many such relationships that fell apart. But it is also a story of accountability, of reconciliation and reconnection. Mei Lin and Pulok's reunion at the end as two old heartbroken couple brings catharsis to the readers. Rita Chowdhury writes emphatically of the embittered hearts of those who had been victims of state incarceration in 1962. Most of them had left for different parts of the world but their trauma had entrenched the deepest parts of their psyche. As she travelled to meet the survivors, she recounts how she had to face initial hostilities and contempt from them. The novel opens in the present, with Anurabh Bora's meeting with Lailin in Hong Kong. Lailin is the daughter of Mie Lin, whom she had given birth in China. Anurag Bora, as the mouthpiece of the author provides a context to how the characters gradually relented, broke their silence and opened their hearts. For them what mattered most was that their story be told.

To put into perspective the condition of the Chinese and envision an optimistic future for them, their existence as a part of the Indian experience must be acknowledged. India as a nation occupies a unique position in the cultural psyche and collective memory of the group that had arrived so many years back and made this country their home. What is significant is that many members of the community share concern about the lack of narratives about the Chinese experience in India particularly the 1962 internment. What they want is an acknowledgment from the Indian Government. In a newspaper article titled "Kolkata's Chinese Community Looks Back At a Detention Camp" Paul Chung, president of the Kolkata-based Indian Chinese Association states "The wounds haven't healed. The suffering has to be acknowledged first for the wounds to be healed. This has never happened". C. Vijayasree writes in the *Introduction to Nation in Imagination* (2007)

> Narratives of nation, one may further argue, operate in multiple time and are necessarily polyphonic. Many voices coming from various and different locations—be it margins, minorities or diasporic communities—jostle for space in the arena of national representation. These

> voices contests, contradict and complement each other, and what results is no cacophony but the essential composite nature of the collectivity called nation. (xii)

The Chinese Community in India is a community that exists in a space of 'in-between' a space full of engagements of identity, politics, nation, and nationalism. Nonetheless, their stories and perspectives are as much a part of the national discourse as any mainstream narrative. Yes, the community grieves the darkest period of their history in India and they look forward to an acknowledgement of this by the state agencies. But most significantly they are open to reconciliation and social acceptance since many of them still reside in India and know no other home. The discourse of nationalism and nationhood which became a part of their very existential identity was the result of the 1962 Indo-China war in which the community was caught in between. They were forced to confront their Chinese ancestry and their outsider status even after decades of co-existence in India. 'Home' as a physical space was no longer the one that they had known for so long; rather 'home' had to be constructed at a designated place where they were deported back by the government. So, they had no control anymore about what they could consider as home, nation, or nationality. Therefore, to understand the dilemma of the Chinese-Indians and their interstitial position one must acknowledge the stories of their checkered history in India.

References

Bhaba, Homi K. *Nation and Narration*, Routledge, 2017, Print.

—— (ed). *The Location of Culture*. New York: Routledge, 1994, 2014. Print.

Chowdhury, Rita. *Chinatown Days*. Macmillan, 2017, Print.

Jeffrey, Alexander C. "Toward a Theory of Cultural Trauma", *Cultural Trauma and Collective Identity*. University of California Press, California, 2004. Print.

Li, Kwai-Yun. *The Palm Leaf Fan and Other Stories*. Tsar Publications, 2006. Print.

Mishra, Sudesh. *Diaspora Criticism*, Edinburgh University Press Ltd., 2006.

Vijayasree, C., Meenakshi Mukherjee, Harish Trivedi, and T. Vijay Kumar, (eds.) *Nation in Imagination*, Orient BlackSwan, 2007, 2012.

Website Sources

http://indianchinese.blogspot.in/Kolkata's Chinese Live In Stateless Sorrow By Gautaman Bhaskaran on October 7, 2015 in Asia Times News & Features, China, South Asia, Asia Times

http://nludelhi.ac.in/download/publication/2015/India%20and%20the%20Challenges%20of%20Statelessness.pdf http://www.ndtv.com/india-news/kolkatas-chinese-community-looks-back-at-a-detention-camp-688234

http://www.guidingstar.ca/Kwai-yun_Li.htm Retrieved on 07th October 2015, *http://www.guidingstar.ca/Kwai-yun_Li.htm*,.LI, Kwai Yun.

Guiding Star, 'Interview with Kwai-Yun Li author of *The Palm Leaf Fan and Other Stories*' March 2, 2007

http://iraimedhi.co.in/book/b5/7.pdf

https://tspace.library.utoronto.ca/bitstream/1807/29477/3/Li_Kwai_Y_20116_MA_thesis.pdf

9

'The Poor of India was a Subject for Research...what a wonderful Country!': Mahasweta Devi Questioning the Concept of Indian Nationhood in *Bhasai Tudu*

Laki Molla and Krishanu Ghosh

The struggle in India would continue so long as a handful of exploiters go on exploiting the labour of the common people for their own ends. It matters little where these exploiters are purely British capitalists, or British and Indians in alliance, or even purely Indians.

On 3 March 1931, twenty days before his martyrdom, Bhagat Singh says this to one of his friends. He emphasizes the weakness of nationalism where the people living in the margins of Indian society are deprived and exploited by elite classes (Habib 30). In 1947, with the disappearance of the British from the administration of India, we get our political freedom, but the task of achieving economic independence, social equality, cultural development, intellectual progress, secular outlook and moral regeneration are the problems we are still encountering. The domination of the elites to the poor helpless peasants remained the same even after the independence. Freedom hardly had any meanings in their life. Resistance against this oppression of the elites is expressed through many revolutions which are not given importance always by the mainstream society. Tebhagha and Naxalite movements are two of these kinds of movements where the peasants revolted against the oppression and injustices of the elites.

As the name indicates Tebhagha movement (sharing by thirds) was centered on the peasant's demand of the two-thirds share of the crops cultivated by their labour in the land of the *jotedars* who were collecting half or even sometimes more of the produced crops before. Andre Beteille argued that in the context of the Tebhaga movement in 1946-47, the *jotedars* came to be perceived as an important component of the agrarian class structure as they provided the peasants with land, seeds, ploughs, plough cattle, some food and little money. The agitation of the peasants was supported by Kisan Sabha,[1] during 1946-47. In order to keep the peasants at their bay, the *jotedars* assumed the role of money lenders, which gave them the power to extort forced labour against the unrecovered debts. They also used the local political leaders and their own private army of musclemen to repress the resistance of the peasants. The intervention of the police and the transformation of power from the British to the Congress Govt. in 1947 worked in the repression of the sharecroppers, who are known in different parts of Bengal with different names like Bargadars or Adhiars, agitation. The barghadars, however, get some advantages during the Left Fronts rule in Bengal. But the 'Operation Bargha' aimed at 'giving land to the tiller', failed without solving the question of the future of the recorded barghadars.

Naxalite movement, which takes its name from the place of its origin in the Naxalbari region of North Bengal, is another peasants upsurge against the landlords and aimed at the distribution of land among the landless poor people. It first initiated as a violent uprising in 1967 in the village of Naxalbari by a section of Communist Party of India (Maoists) (CPM) led by Kanu Sanyal and Jangal Santhal and later expanded to many districts of West Bengal and Andhra Pradesh, mostly in forested areas, where the people are exploited by contractors, local politicians, and local bureaucrats. Like Tebhaga Movement, here also the society is divided into two parts—in one hand we have the landless peasants and on the other the elite who have the support of the politicians and government. The Left front was supporting the cause of the peasants. But there are doubts about their actual purpose of upholding the deprived condition of the peasants. Sumit Sarkar, about the Tebhaga movement, observed:

> The memorandum of the Bengal Provincial Kisan Sabha submitted to the land Revenue (Flood) Commission in 1939 had included a section on sharecroppers' grievances, but specific reforms it proposed mainly related to the central demand of abolition of zamindari, and said nothing about enhancing the *bargadar* share of the crop to two-thirds (tebhaga). Nor did it mention the tankha (produce rent) issue in Mymensingh, or landlord tolls on 'haats' (rural market). Yet the powerful movements of the poor peasant-cum-sharecroppers that communists were able to organise in the 1940s were precisely around tankha, market exactions (baat tola) in North Bengal in 1939-40 and of course tebhaga in 1946-47. (XLV)

After the Independence, the assumption of centre-margin binarism is changed. The elite Indian secured the position of the centre, but the tribal and the subalterns remain in the peripheral position without any kind of significant development in their condition. The role of the British is now assumed by the elites who began to exploit them in different ways. It can be explained through the 'Internal Colonial Model' of Michael Hechter where 'core is seen to dominate the periphery politically and to exploit it materially'. In the 'Internal Colonial Model', there is the emergence of 'advanced' and 'less advanced' groups owing to the 'unequal distribution of resources and power'. This leads to the 'cultural division of labour' where the members of the more powerful group—the core occupy the prestigious social roles and denied the access of the less advanced groups to these roles through the 'institutionalization of the existing stratification system' (9). This cultural division of labour "leads individuals to identify themselves with their groups and contributes to the development of distinctive ethnic identification" (Ozkirimili 80) which paves the path for group solidarity. Another important reason for its emergence is the substantial economic inequalities between these two groups which are seen by the members of the less advanced group as a part of a pattern of collective oppression. Adequate communication among the members of the oppressed groups certainly initiated this process. And thus "there exists the probability that the disadvantaged group will, in time, reactively assert its own culture as equal or superior to that of the relatively advantaged core. This may help it conceive of itself as a separate 'nation' and seek independence" (Hechter 10). The elites in India created a simulated colonial situation through the practice of bonded slavery, land displacement and physical torture and created a situation in which it became impossible for the tribals to reach the level of the elites. These elites are also helped by the government and its police. The government launches many welfare projects for the development of the tribals, but they never implement them. The mainstream literature also neglects the issues of the tribals. Mahasweta Devi's novels are an attack against these attitudes of the elites as well as the government towards these landless peasants and question the homogeneous totalizing concept of a unified nation.

Bashai Tudu is a novel centred on the lives of the title character who like Kuber in *Padma Nadir Majhi* (The Boatman of the River Padma)[2] represents the macrocosmic world of a particular community who are constantly cheated by the mainstream society as well as the resistance and armed revolt of these helpless peasants. Covering a period between 1967 and 1977, it is a story about the fierce agrarian Revolution mainly by the landless labourers in Naxalbari region in the north of Bengal. The Estate Acquisition Act of 1954 limited the landholding capacity of individuals to 25 acres. The zamindar, jotedars and big landowners paid no heed to this rule and ruthlessly suppressed the struggle of the landless labourers demand of getting the minimum wages prescribed by the government. These poor labourers are not even favoured by the government. The government policies have a very little role in their daily life. Rather it the hunger, not the government that regulates their lives. In his conversation with Kali Santra, Bashai presents the plight of these landless peasants:

> They were aware of the glory that the MW law had brought to the government, how it had redeemed the administration's sense of guilt, how it had been a topic for discussion at several meetings held in air-conditioned chambers over steaming cups of Nescafé, and how it had drawn a blank in implementation. As with the naked and the hungry the world over, the lives of the Santals are determined and regulated by hunger, not by any government. Hunger rules as a tyrant, keeping its subjects always on the run. Hence the Santals never staked their claims for the MW, and preferred to work, on daily wages or for contracted sums, for the landlords—sowing, raising and reaping the aush, the aman, the boro, the IR8, gram, pigeon pea, mustard, and jute. (Devi 61)

Thus, the peasants did not care for the minimum wage the government has fixed for their labour because they are quite aware of the fact that the landlords are not going to pay them the wages though the government made it 'mandatory'. The laws were made only because they have to be made and they need never be enforced and that those for whom the laws are made need never reap the benefits. No political parties, even the Communist Kisan Sabha, are not concerned about it. No parties want to come in conflict with the jotedars because the support of the jotedars works as a driving force to keep the government in power. The government and the jotedars are 'lovely doveys'. Thus while the interests of the jotedars are supported and their oppressive reign is sanctioned, the rights of the tribal peasants are deprived. Bashai expresses his deep anger at every political parties' attitude towards those who raise their voice against the authority. The sentence is also full of deep indignation:

> Before we were born, whoever challenged authority would be branded terrorists; then they were called Congressites. When the Congress came to power they were branded Communists. Now the Front calls them Naxalites. That's what they'll call me. Doesn't matter to me in the least. How can one show the truth to one who feigns blindness? (Devi 49)

Bashai Tudu, the protagonist of the novel was once an active member of the Communist Party but he becomes a rebel when the party neglected the six words—'statutory minimum wages for agricultural labourers'. The hollowness of the Communists is bitterly expressed in the words of Bashai,

> The babus are a caste by themselves like the Bagdis, and the Kaoras, yes, a caste. And that's why such a good man like you have to take your stand with the babus only because you are a babu yourself. And then in the party study circle you would give us lectures on the class struggle. (Devi 24)

The Kisan Sabha and the Communist Party that acquired a special Indian character in Indian soil also came to follow the law of the ladder: rise a rung and forget the lower rung. This law is persistent in every field of Indian experience—in religion, politics, business, education, culture and even in personal life.

To keep the labourers at their control the jotedars assumed the role of a moneylender who is not at all concerned whether the harvest is good or the yield is lower. The lower yield has a direct impact on the plight of the share croppers and agricultural labourers. When the yield is lower, they are driven to borrow both paddy and cash from the jotedar-cum-moneylenders and here the moneylender uses his weapon of interest charged at compound rates and makes a small landowner either a landless agricultural labourer or a migrant labour. The role of the government in this regard is presented in an ironic manner by the novelist:

> In a democracy the government would never violate the fundamental right of a small peasant to be victimized by his jotedar or his moneylender. The Indian Constitution respected every citizen's fundamental right to become whatever he could by dint of his guts. The poor therefore had the right to become poorer still. A peasant today had the right to be a landless agricultural labourer tomorrow. There was no governmental agency or strong organization to stand by these men who made a living by cultivating other people's land. The government and the official peasant organizations were within their

democratic rights to deny any kind of support to these people. (Devi 87)

With the government support the jotedars, instead of giving the compulsory MW to the labourers threaten them with the fear of hiring migrant labourers to work in their field. And if any labourer turns the offer of the landlord down to work depriving the local agricultural labourers, he is amused by both the landlord as well as the government. The landlord calls him 'the tribe of pious Yudhisthira' and the government marks him as 'politically potent' in its official records. The jotedars even enjoy the government funds allotted for the tribal welfare. In the novel funds allotted for the fresh construction of the peasant houses destroyed in the floods are utilised to build a pucca go down for Pratap Golder's rice and paddy. The allotted funds for a Health Centre in Bannari went into the construction of a proper road for trucks to carry Pratap's rice and paddy. Thus, besides depriving the peasants their actual wages, the jotedars also forfeits the money allotted for the tribals by the government and pushed them to more poverty and increases the difference between these two classes. They are even not concerned about the minimum wage rate and 10% of them had no idea about the independence of the country like Bibhutibhusan Bandopadhyay's Bhanumati[3] who does not know where the Bharatvarsh is. They are forced to believe that when a man is born as a tribal he inherits deprivation. No upper caste Hindu can ever share the same source of deprivation. The dark tribal was the first child of a dark India.

Partha Chatterjee while tracing the various stages of the Indian National Movement, points out the 'neo-colonial mask' in the relationship between the elites and the masses whose support was appropriated by both Gandhi and Nehru during the Independence, but afterwards kept outside the national framework of politics (Chatterjee 125). Even during the colonial era, the struggles of the tribals are not given importance by the dominant historiography. They termed their contribution as "supplement" to the original narratives of the nations and nationalism which can be easily "forgotten" (Bagchi 43). The Subaltern Studies Group points out their negative aspects of the homogeneous and holistic nationalism. Ranjit Guha criticizes the way in which historians like Anil Seal dismissed the peasant uprisings and agrarian agitation as "old fashioned" and "unimportant". Guha argues that we need to put the popular resistance firmly outside politics so that the role of Indians as collaborators with the British can be stressed rather than mere participants in the act of resistance against the British (Guha 299).

Mahasweta Devi in her preface to the novel points out how for a long time Bengali literature indulged in the denial of the reality and has been suffered by an atrophy of conscience. As the writers refuse to see 'the writing on the wall', the conscientious reader is turning away from them. It is surprising that the writers living in a country tormented with so many problems—social injustice, communal discord and evil customs—should fail to find material for their work in their own country and people. Such Indifference to people can only be possible, perhaps, in a semi-colonial, semi-feudal country like India, still suffering from the hangover of foreign rule. Going against those writers ignoring the issues and rights of the oppressed, Mahasweta Devi argues that a conscientious writer should take a firm stand in defence of the exploited, otherwise he or she will never be absolved by history.

Notes

1. All India Kisan Sabha was the name of the peasants front of the undivided Communist Party of India, an important peasant movement formed by Sahajanand Saraswati in 1936. It later split into two organisations known by the same name: AIKS (Ajoy Bhavan) and AIKS (Ashoka Road).
2. *Padma Nadir Majhi* (The Boatman of the River Padma) is a Bengali novel written by Manik Bandopadhyay in 1936.
3. Bhanumati is a character found in Bengali novelist Bibhutibhushan Bandyopadhyay's novel *Aranyak*.

References

Bagchi, Alaknanda. "Conflicting Nationalisms: The Voice of the Subaltern in Mahasweta Devi's *Bashai Tudu*." *Tulsa Studies in Women's Literature*, vol. 15, no. 1, 1996, pp. 41-50. *JSTOR*, www.jstor.org/stable/463971. Accessed 15 Jan. 2020.

Chatterjee, Partha. *Nationalist Thought and the Colonial World: A Derivative Discourse*. Zed Books, 1993.

D. Bandyopadhyay. "Tebhaga Movement in Bengal: A Retrospect." *Economic and Political Weekly*, vol. 36, no. 41, 2001, pp. 3901-907. *JSTOR*, www.jstor.org/stable/4411230. Accessed 15 Jan. 2020.

Devi, Mahasweta. *Bashai Tudu*. Translated by Samik Bandyopadhyay and Gayatri Chakraborty Spivak, Thema, 1990.

Guha, Ranjit. *Subaltern Studies VI: Writing on South Asian History and Society*. OUP, 1989.

Habib, S. Irfan. *Indian Nationalism: The Essential Writings*. Aleph, 2017.

Hechter, Michael. *Internal Colonialism: The Celtic fringe in British National Development, 1536-1966*. University of California Press, 1975.

Ozkirimili, Umat. *Theories of Nationalism: A Critical Introduction*. 2nd edition, Palgrave Macmillan, 2010.

10

Nationalism and History in Birendra Kumar Bhattacharya's *Love in the Time of Insurgency* and Gabriel Garcia Marquez's *One Hundred Years of Solitude*

Satya Nath Pegu

Introduction

Nationalism is a sentiment of unity among a set of people occupying a particular territory, born out of common factors such as language, religion, economy, and administrative system. Nationalism, when it becomes synonymous with pure patriotism will prove a unique blessing to humanity and to the world but at the same time, it can also be terrifying and a hurdle to the universal civilization as it glorifies its own nation, stands for unity and solidarity of its own nation and leads to hatred of other countries. Nationalism makes people self-confined. They generally talk in terms of their own nation only. Nationalism also gives rise to imperialism; a source of continued violence and oppression. As scholars of nationalism from different schools of thoughts have argued, the conception of a nation and construction of national identity are inexorably related to a people's imagining of their history. History is a significant influence on their nationalism and patriotism. There is an obvious sense in which nationalist mobilization has an important basis in images of the past: images which are typically embellished to produce a tendentious image of the community's own history.

Individuals are misinformed about their national history, and official narratives and propaganda frequently mischaracterize it. In the contemporary period, literature from the world critically examines the representations of marginalized history among different ethnic communities. It is due to the impact of colonial culture, migration and globalization which distort the authenticity of history of nation. It hybridizes the indigenous history and also excludes the identity of a particular community. The new historical approach produces difference, fractured and doubled identity that leads to form selfhood and subjectivity in reorganizing indigenous history, language, religion and culture. E.J. Hobsbawm in his groundbreaking work, *Nations and Nationalism Since 1780: Programme, Myth and Reality* comments that ethnicity and territorial power or sovereignty are two important ingredients of a modern nation. By the term ethnicity he means a common descent, history and language and the term territorial power or sovereignty as the capacity form an independent state. He also pays ample attention to the social and political developments in the later part of the 20th century as determining factors for a nation.

In Northeast Indian English literature, history and nationalism issues are juxtaposed with the distinct linguistic, cultural, and religion among different ethnic communities. The assimilation and the impact of western culture exclude the indigenous identity of the tribes. So, Freedom Movement leads to violence and insurgency. It produces a troubled political climate. Birendra Kumar Bhattacharya's *Love in the Time of Insurgency* (1960) presents the struggle for history and identity among the Nagas during the World War II. It clearly interprets the disintegration of Naga society against the impact of western education and religion. The characters challenge the dominant national identity with different political strategies in the form of insurgency and violence. Bhattacharya significantly brings out the formation of Naga militancy and armed struggle of his time. The story is set in Ukhrul, a Tankhul Naga village during the turbulent period of World War II. The novel covers a span of five years beginning with the invasion of the Japanese Army and ending by the time of assassination of Mahatma Gandhi in Indian history. Latin American fiction explores the history of colonial dominants over the Latin American countries. Europeans like Spain, Portugal and Italy dominated Latin America in which Latin America lost their indigenous culture. The Civil War and the Cuban Revolution alter the history and identity in the region. These factors influenced the writers to re-examine history, identity, culture and tradition from different perspectives. The major events of Columbian history are the pre-Hispanic life, the Civil Wars, Conflict between the Conservatives and the Liberals, Banana Massacre etc. *One Hundred Years of Solitude* (1967) is organized into three narrative blocs: the utopian foundation of the town of Macondo; the town's consolidation, the development, the expansion and the onset of crisis, and its destruction. It reflects the history of Columbia since independence. Through the establishment of the Buendia family in the imaginary town of Macondo, Gabriel Garcia Marquez shows the struggle for a national identity. The story of Buendia family is a metaphor for the history of the continent since independence. The sense of collective nationhood has not been properly formed due to oligarchic control in Latin American countries after the Spanish domination. The lack of grass-roots participation or any form of democratic means is the factor of political instabilities. In this context, the story of Macondo allegorically parallels the foundation, consolidation and eventual violent decline of the Columbian national state.

Objectives

The aim of this paper is to trace out the distorted history and the influence of nationalism in Birendra Kumar Bhattacharya's *Love in the Time of Insurgency* and Gabriel Garcia Marquez's *One Hundred Years of Solitude*. Attempt will also be made to bring out the political strategies such as violence and oppression in the select novels.

Methodology

The study is based on both primary and secondary data. It includes texts and critical references. Both the sources are collected to analyze the proposed study in detail.

Hypothesis

In the twentieth century, nationalism and history are relevant issues in the contemporary literature. The post-independence period examines the transformation of ethnic identity and history. It is due to the dominance of Western narrative that displaced history in the form of linguistic, religion and culture. So, the ethnic consciousness draws out the difference, fracture and multiple identities and history in the postcolonial time. Different oppositional values and beliefs strive to bring out their distorted history and identity in the form of violence, extortion and insurgency.

Discussion

In *Love in the Time of Insurgency*, different political strategies are adopted among the characters to form new ethnic identity against the transforming forces. The oppositional ideologies bring disastrous consequences in the name of Freedom Movement. The impact of World War II, the western education, the Gandhian ideals and Christianity fractured the indigenous identity among the Naga society. It forms an idea of difference from the earlier identity and draws a consciousness within the identity seekers. Rishang's idea of freedom movement is based on Gandhian and the Christianity ideals. Rishang's ideologies for identity movement are different from Videsselie, while Videsselie idea of freedom movement deals with militancy and violence. In order to resist the difference and doubled identities, the characters stick on the idea of selfhood. This destablishes the repressed and marginalized identity. Bhattacharya textualized the non-literary elements to resituate the past history of the Naga society. The non-literary elements like, World War II and the ideals of Indian Freedom Movement are set as backdrop of the novel to reinterpret the marginalized identity. The political ideologies of Videsselie and Rishang are discursive that break the monolithic views of ethnic identity. Different ideologies set up multiple discourses in contesting the dominant power and politics. There is a struggle to change the rigid construction and hegemony of the national identity against the small ethnic communities. Ngazek along with Videsselie opposed the universalization of Christian religion in the Naga village and exclaimed:

> The Nagas need a different kind of freedom. The Christianity and modern education have taken us on the wrong path. I want neither the white men nor the black men. I have no love for the Japanese either. The Nagas were happier when they were naked. (Bhattacharya Birendra Kumar, 15)

Such ideologies of political identities create conflict among the same ethnic community. Ngazek feels marginalized when Rishang and some members are willing to adopt the western education and Christian religion. But Rishang's desire to gives natives western education and ideologies, repress Ngazek's views on identity movement. After the end of empire internal conflict prevails. While contesting this dominance, there is a power struggle to transform the existing power of politics.

Bhattacharya's narrative on identity juxtaposes the difference of past and present of the Tankhul Naga. Everything of the past is textualized. History is represented in to a new one, which is excluded in the past. It takes historical, political and social events as co-texts. The narrative is non-linear in presenting all the incidents. Judging the historical truths, it negotiates selfhood by drawing comparison between the past and present. The factors relating to these are education, religion and war. Rishang in Calcutta absorbs Gandhian ideals of Freedom Movement. The meeting addressed by Gandhi makes him acknowledge the ideologies that are more appropriate in contrast to the violence of Videsselie. Not only Gandhian ideal, but Rishang's education in Calcutta leads him to change his perception towards Naga freedom movement. It alternates the dominant ideologies of the time. But Videsselie is unable to accept Rishang's philosophy on identity struggle which is different from the native norms. Such opposite ideologies of Rishang and Videsselie create internal rivalry between them. The Gandhian ideals of Rishang are rejected by Videsselie because the national identity mispresents the regional identity. This influences Videsselie to form an oppositional force. The author's alternate analysis is a project to represent the consciousness of minority community. In

Nation and Narration, it is mentioned "attention to those easily obscured, but highly significant, recesses of the national culture from which alternative constituencies of people and oppositional analytic capacities may emerge youth, the everyday, nostalgia, 'new ethnicities', new social movements, 'the politics of difference'—and assign new meanings and different directions to the process of historical change" (Bhabha, H.K. 03). The novel examines how national discourse and national movement homogenize the regional identity without acknowledging the difference. Bhattacharya's narrative significantly reflects the voice of the marginalized. Reconstituting ethnic identity, there is also ambivalence in Videsselie's ideologies. At another situation, when Videsselie is asked to join in the mainstream national movement, he hesitates to surrender. It forms subjectivity and selfhood to protect the eroding identity from the threat of in-between identity. The consciousness of the self-alters the rigid national identity in which a particular ethnic community contests to deconstruct.

Religion plays a dominant role in shaping identity of the characters. The impact of Christianity creates a religious rivalry among the people and divides as Christian and non-Christian. At one level, it inspires peace and cultivates humanistic values. It also changes the evil mindsets of the natives. Yangmasa, Rishang's father and Dr. Brock plead to build the church, but this is severely opposed by the non-Christians Ngathinkhui, Ngazek and other members of the village. Rishang motivates the people to follow Christian ideals. But Ngazek does not approve his son's marriage to a Christian girl. Bhattacharya highlights how religion is an instrument in restoring disintegration in the freedom struggle. Rishang's acceptance of Christian religion symbolizes the passive resistance towards freedom and Videsselie's violence represents active protests against the dominant ideals. Rishang used Christian ideals to mould peace in the society, but it is politicized when Rishang rejects evangelical works of Dr. Brock to move against Videsselie's politics of guerrilla war.

War brings great severity in the small village, Tangkhul. It changes peaceful co-existence of the particular region. The Japanese attack and the China-Burma war threatened the natives.

Allied bombing destroyed everything in sight and rendered the villagers homeless. The war also influenced the youths to join in the Allied force. The native resists such influence and its impact. So, Ngazek opposed his son, Khating's joning in Army. The war converts the youths of the natives to follow the violent ideologies. It divides and displaces the natives of the small village. Besides the violence of identity, the novel historicizes its existence. Sharengla becomes an object of the Japanese soldier. She was kidnapped and sexually abused during the war. From this perspective, the natives turn aggressive towards outsiders. The violence of war also influences Videsselie and his men in which they protest with arms and ammunitions in the name of freedom. On the other hand, passive resistance of Rishang follows the ideals of education and religion in the war trodden zone. Countering the fractured identity, the characters' consciousness brings out difference and contradictions.

The crisis of Naga insurgency movement is very complex among the provinces of Northeast region. The basic problems of the tribal found in the northeast are fearful domination and exploitation. It is not only a political problem, but it is also related to human problem. At other times, some are restricted, politically isolated and neglected. Question of equality and the consciousness of indigenousness formed several insurgency movement. In the insurgency movement, an individual and the society are exploited. It creates imbalance due to several atrocities meted out by the revolutionary group. Violence, jealousy and betrayal arouse in among the people.

Gabriel Garcia Marquez reference to "pig-tail" in *One Hundred Years of Solitude* presents the history of Columbia back to the days of the discovery of America by Columbus. The family narrative that Garcia Marquez tells not only about Jose Arcadio and Ursula, but also of all Latin America that takes Columbus's account of a race of pig-tailed men as its moment of origin. Columbus' myth of a race of pig-tailed men becomes in Garcia Marquez, a similar story of origin for Latin America. *One Hundred Years of Solitude* tells a myth about the birth in which it is not of man as biological being, but as a culture. So, in this cultural birth narrative, it is believed that Latin America is born out of the union of two people and their culture. In its infancy, Jose Arcadio Buendia's Macondo resembles a Chibcha chiefdom. The life in Macondo is as peaceful as that of a Chibcha clan before the advent of Spanish. As the Chieftain of the group, Jose Arcadio Buendia emphasized to maintain the harmony of the village. But the arrival of Melquiades and Don Apolinar Moscote bring catastrophe to Macondo. The creation of Macondo on the model of Chibcha clan symbolizes Marquez's yearning for the return of pre-hispanic life to Columbia. When Macondo was established, the founding people were full of optimism and hope. They leave their original homeland with a view to find a new town near the sea. The marriage of Jose Arcadio Buendia and Ursula Iguarana was scandalized because they were relatives. People believed that their offspring would be cursed and be born with pig's tail. This unfortunate situation led Jose Arcadio Buendia to kill Prudencio Aguilar to defend his honour. Though the killing is later legitimized as a duel of honour, the ghost of Prudencio Aguilar haunts him. So, Jose Arcadio Buendia with his wife left the town and founded a new one to live without their past. To analyze Macondo as a nation in this light can be compared to the time when a nation first comes to exist, develop and encounter. The Buendia family and their hometown Macondo become a stage where Gabriel Garcia Marquez shows the history of the colonization of his nation. The appearance of Macondo in Jose Arcadio's dream symbolically reveals that Macondo itself serves as a mirror, reflecting its emergence of the real nation of Columbia.

After its independence, there was a political conflict between the Conservatives and the Liberals and they struggled for absolute power. It resulted in the War of a Thousand Days and *La Violencia*. Marquez's novel is a product of history in which it actively participates in making history. History plays an important role in constructing nationhood where war and violence become part of Columbian history. War and violence yield a disparate impact in Columbia. It marks an oppressive regime and conveys a sense of vicious circle. The repetitious wars between the Conservatives and the Liberals defined no absolute progress. The arrival of Don Apolinar Moscote, a magistrate appointed from Bogota to govern Macondo reflects the futility of the two parties: the Conservatives and the Liberals. This is found when Colonel Aureliano Buendia felt aware of the ideological differences between the two parties since the boundaries between the two are vague. Colonel Aureliano Buendia and his leftist supporters roamed in the various regions of Columbia and tried to revolt against the oppressive regime. He asked his nephew Arcadio, the champion of the Liberals causes, to impose order upon Macondo. Arcadio was a cruel ruler who killed Don Apolinar Moscote though Remedios Moscote was his aunt and daughter of Don Apolinar Moscote. This led Colonel Aureliano Buendia to feel the blurred boundaries between the two parties and recognized that people fight for their ideologies are absurds. For the Conservatives and the Liberals, pride brings an inferiority and superiority that leads to dominate the weaker. Colonel Aureliano Buendia felt that until both the parties remove their arrogance, the war will not end.

The pride and power of the two political parties are the subversion in their shaped ideologies. The innocent people fanatically followed their leaders in ignorance where they were totally marginalized in knowing the truth of ideology. Garcia Marquez portrays the crooked nature of the two parties before the people of his nation. The novel depicts the necessity to end the meaningless politics and to form an identity that is relevant to the nation. The reconstruction of events related to the two major political parties will bring the people to light, who would strive for the unity of the people and make their nation march towards a new identity. As new historicists linked past and present, social, political and economic issues, Garcia Marquez represents all these episodes in the form of literary presentation in his novels.

Gabriel Garcia Marquez reconstructs the events of the episodes of Banana Strike and military repression in *One Hundred Years of Solitude*. He re-situated the past to form a new entity by juxtaposing historical anecdotes. The repressed history and subjugation of the past are brought to light where history is textualized. Like new historicism, the aim of cultural materialism is to allow the literary text to recover its histories which previous kinds of study have often ignored. It highlights oppression of the rural poor, state power and resistance to it. The banana incident with a vengeance portrays the true history that was manipulated by the authorities of the Banana Company and the government. Garcia Marquez demystifies the history of the subcontinent by rewriting the incidents of the Banana Company. It exposes the ruling establishment's tradition of manipulating history. Aureliano Buendia, brought up by his uncle regards that Macondo is the victim of the Banana Company's imperialist exploitation, discovers that school history books portray the company as a benefactor which brought prosperity and progress. But, Garcia Marquez debunks official myths by offering an alternative history.

In *One Hundred Years of Solitude*, Garcia Marquez deconstructs the representation of Banana Company as the benefactor in the school history book that brought prosperity and progress to the country. Because of the US interest, army did not support Columbia. This is what Garcia Marquez wants to alternate the history of his nation. During the Banana Strike, government betrayed its own people. It is the consequences of this particular incident that led Garcia Marquez to reveal the truth in *One Hundred Years of Solitude*. The juxtaposition of this incident is to remove the conspiracy of silence of the past. The Columbian elites were the people that suppressed the truth from the collective memory of the people. Being Columbian elite, Garcia Marquez rectified the truth of history and its people. He connects past episodes of various places and time with minute details and delineates how such violent issue are products of place and time he belong to. By doing this, he wants to bring something new to the Columbian nation of Latin America.

Conclusion

Birendra Kumar Bhattacharya's *Love in the Time of Insurgency* and Gabriel Garcia Marquez's *One Hundred Years of Solitude* examine the factors relating to violence and oppression while shaping the idea of nation. Due to the impact of colonial culture, indigenous history and identity got transformed. In this process, there is an exclusion of language, religion, custom and culture of particular ethnic community. This creates consciousness against one's nation to reform the difference with political ideologies. Insurgency and War are the dominant factors in national movement. It shapes identity in the form of militancy and violence. At another level, identity emerges with monolithic principles of the nations. So, the opposite forces in identity movement establish crisis. In the novel *Love in the Time of Insurgency*, Birendra Kumar Bhattacharya explores opposite political ideologies between Rishang and Videsseli. Rishang's strategy is based on Gandhian philosophy and Videsselie deals with Subhas Bose. Videsselie counters with insurgency and violence. In the name of freedom, it is not only disintegrating the natives, but also their unity in participating in the freedom struggle. Birendra Kumar Bhattacharya examined the regional identities that is overlapped by the national identity. After the end of empire, there is an internal conflict in terms of religion, class, caste and culture. There is a confrontation between the dominant group and the marginalized group. Though, the colonized country is free from the colonizers, the ideologies are still prevalent. In the novel, the western ideologies are manifested in the natives where it creates an ambivalence. The author historicizes the Naga identity movement as a microcosm of larger political reality in India. The figure of Gandhi's struggle is shown through the character of Rishang and the socio-political turmoil is reflected with Naga insurgency movement. Gabriel Garcia Marquez's *One Hundred Years of Solitude* shows an unethical political organization in the history of Columbia as well as Latin America. *One Hundred Years of Solitude* highlights that neither the Conservatives nor the Liberals manage to gain foothold in Colombian politics as if time did not yield any progress and Columbia was stagnant with its political whirlpool that has grown with violence and bloodshed. The negative sense of unproductiveness is found in the dialogue between Colonel Aureliano Buendia and his mother, Ursula when he perceived that the town of Macondo has changed since he left to fight for the liberal cause. Jose Arcadio Buendia, Ursula's husband also experiences the same feeling. Garcia Marquez juxtaposed the dark side of the civil wars and made his people understand that unless they wriggle out of the menace of the civil wars, it is impossible for them to achieve national identity. Thus, it reconstructs the past so that his people can carve out a new identity in near future for their nation. The discursive formation of the ideology brings hopelessness to Colonel Aureliano Buendia. His self-policing in his activities ends with an absurdity. It is a self-destruction without any definite progress. There are repression, violence and exploitation in the history of Latin America. The powerful authority and the marginalized historical agendas are brought to light in examining the distortion and manipulation in national history. However, the authors deconstruct violence and militant practices in representing their nations. The narratives give a voice to the underrepresented region. It reinterprets the national discourse in which the marginalized identities are homogenized. Thus, it counters colonialism as well as other kinds of political or cultural hegemony often imposed on the smaller identities by the nation state.

Works Cited

Anderson, Benedict. *Imagined Communities: Reflections on the Origin and Spread of Nationalism,* London: Verso, 1991. Print.

Bell-Villada, Gene H. *Marquez: The Man and His Work*. Chapel Hill: The University of North Carolina Press, 2010. Print.

Bhabha, H.K. *Nation and Narration*. London: Routledge, 1990. Print.

Bhattacharya, Birendra Kumar. *Love in the Time of Insurgency.* New Delhi: Katha, 2005. Print.

Brannigan, John. *New Historicism and Cultural Materialism*. 1998. New York: Palgrave Macmillan, 2017. Print.

Deka, Umesh. *Post-War Assamese Novel*. Guwahati: Chandra Prakash, 2008. Print.

Erikson, E.H. *Identity Crisis*. New York: Norton, 1975. Print.

Hobsbawm, E.J. ed. *Nations and Nationalism Since 1780: Programme, Myth, Reality.* New Delhi: CUP, 1990. Print.

Marquez, Gabriel Garcia. *One Hundred Years of Solitude*. Trans. Gregory Rabassa. London: Penguin, 1996. Print.

Nuh, V.K. *Struggle for Identity in North-East India*. Guwahati: Spectrum Publications, 2001. Print.

Simson, J.A., and Weiner, E.S. eds. *The Oxford English Dictionary*. Oxford: Clarendon Press, 1989. Print.

11

Oscillating between House and Home in Jhumpa Lahiri's *The Namesake*

Tarulata Pegu

The present paper explores the recurrent topics of belongingness, otherness, in-between, space, and hybridity that are located in Jhumpa Lahiri's *The Namesake* (2003). The characters and their identity formation are analyzed through the aforementioned theoretical frameworks. The Indo-American writer, Jhumpa Lahiri as a diasporic writer recounts the Indian culture, tradition, memories, ethnicity etc. and thus reflects the nationalistic spirit through her work. The objective of the paper is to trace how Lahiri's characters oscillate between house and home, and further searches for an escape to a 'third home'. Concepts given by Henry Lefebvre, bell hooks, Salman Rushdie, and Homi Bhabha are brought in to analyze the novel.

bell hooks (1952), pseudonym of Gloria Jean Watkins, the African American author, in her books like *Yearning: Race, Gender and Cultural Politics* (1990), *Bone Black: Memories of Girlhood* (1996), and *Belonging: A Culture of Place* (2009) exposes the difficulties experienced by diasporic African-American intellectuals like her in western cultures. These American rural people, as she mentioned in her book *Belonging*, still suffers the class injustice. Her ancestors suffered the trauma of slavery and segregation. She tried to recount these unrecognized and the poignant memories in her essays. Her most notable lines of the *Yearning* are, "memory need not be passive reflection, a nostalgic longing for things to be as they once were; it can function as a way of knowing and learning from the past", and "serves to illuminate and transform the present" (*Yearnings*, 40, 147).

Her most popular work where she raises the question of 'belonging' is *Bone Black: Memories of Girlhood*. The work sketches her memories of the past combined with imagination and dreams. She recounts those events that left a deep impact on her mind and how those still influences her at present. It narrates how as a black girl she saw the world and the community she belonged. Right from her childhood she experienced the sense of loneliness and fear, and she was incomprehensive of her world. She has a rebellious spirit to shatter everything on its way and had the ardent desire for belongingness. Throughout her works she celebrates the black southern folk and culture and delves back to it time and again. She has experienced the bitter taste of being in a segregated school, and she faces discrimination within home. Her only place of belonging that she found in her childhood was books which would later give her the credit of being a successful writer. Thus, there are recurrent emphasis on alienation and a constant yearning for belonging in bell hooks.

Henri Lefebvre's pioneering work on space, everyday life, urban theory, geography and cultural studies among others added to his growing fame as a writer. His notable work *Production of Space*, published in the early 1970s, discusses the concept of 'space' which bypasses geography. 'Space' denotes the process of "urbanization and globalization: as at every scale new geographies have developed" (Schmid 28). Here 'city' and 'space' lay on a single sort as a spatial process. 'Space' is famously considered as a social product, which does not exist independently "in itself". Rather, according to Lefebvre, it is bonded with social reality and is therefore a social product in specific society.

Lefebvre further gave importance to human beings in his analysis of materialist theory. Human beings with all their imaginations and beliefs involves in activities that integrates them with each other. The moments in 'production of space' can be divided into three interconnected processes. They are—the "perceived" space related to everyday social life, the "conceived" space, which is the theoretical concepts for intellectuals, and last the "lived" space where human beings live through their imagination and this is reflected in arts and literature. The third space has the capacity to go beyond and reframe the other two spaces. In order to understand the relationship across territories and their cultural meaning he employs the "lived" space and experiences.

In his title essay "Imaginary Homelands" (1991), Salman Rushdie gave his views regarding migration and its aftermath as experienced by people. The essay describes how there is always an agony to dive back into one's roots. These emigrants desire a "homeland" where they can claim their belonging. Salman Rushdie, born in India, migrated to Pakistan and shifted finally to New York, feels insecure about his belongingness. He always looks forward to India as his roots as it is where the deeper values of life he learnt. India with its cultures and values left a deep imprint on his mind. Residing in a foreign country a sense of loss always haunts him. Other diasporic writers, along him and Lahiri, cannot claim their belonging to the past even if they wish. It is uneasy for them to adapt to the present as the past memories would intrude them. They find themselves trapped between two nations, two languages and two cultures. Therefore they imagine themselves in a third 'imaginary homeland'.

New theories of 'in-between identities' were brought into the works of postcolonial theorists such as Gayatri Spivak and Homi Bhabha. Bhabha has strongly called for the manifestation of the 'in-between'. This in-between, according to him, is "the creative, malleable indeterminacy involving feelings of simultaneous repulsion and the desire that exists at the interface between self and the other" (Waugh 355). In other words, it means existing in between the divergence of the two unequal worlds with repulsion or indifference simultaneously. In his influential essay "Of Mimicry and Man" (1985), he deals with his much discussed topic of 'hybridization'. He employs it to bring in the point that the Colonizer tried to remake an image of themselves out of the colonized. The colonized realizing the 'not-quite sameness' feels distorted because of his failure to become the complete white man and also they lost their original version of themselves which always leads to what Bhabha calls hybridization. Following the path of Rushdie, another important concept forward by him, is the 'third space'. It is related to migration of minority communities where they hybridize with the metropolitan culture and space, and concerns how they are included into it. So, the 'third space' is the vicinity where "cultural interaction and mutual intervention in metropolitan urban space" takes place, especially between the migrant and the natives (Waugh 356).

Thus Jhumpa Lahiri, born to Indian-immigrant parents in London, moved to American at an early age and settled down in Italy, shares the same sense of alienation and lack of belongingness with the above-mentioned authors. She has dealt with this "rootedness" and "uprooted", experienced by her characters extensively, in *The Namesake*.

Ashima, in the novel, truly searches for a 'third imaginary home'. As formulated by Rushdie, she creates an imaginary home for herself without borders (as her name suggests) and like hooks, she deeply pines for her past life. The simple definition of "House" is given by the *Merriam Webster Dictionary* as a building that serves as living quarters, "House" is made a "Home" with a congenial environment by a family living together.

Ashima is exposed to a sense of loss about her Indian heritage and culture, soon after her marriage, as she moves to America with her husband Ashoke. She felt abandoned and lonely when she was pregnant with her first child. She has nothing much to do in the foreign land. This made her terribly miss her home in Kolkata. To pass her hours, she used to read dozen times the "Desh Magazine" that she has brought with her. Moreover, her father's work on the magazine connects her to him. She recreates the food habits of India. In America, she often makes a mixture of salted peanuts and sprouts that were available in Kolkata sidewalks. After the birth of her son Gogol, she complained her husband that, "...I don't want to raise Gogol alone in this country. It's not right. I want to go back" (Lahiri 33). She imagines how things would have been different in her homeland. All the family members and relatives would have joined hands to raise the child. What pained her most of all was the lost letter that her grandmother had sent from India with a name to be given to her son. She found opportunities to cry at every small thing. This made her husband guilty of bringing his wife in a foreign land. But another vital fact of his life would not let him to go back to India. He remembered how Mr. Ghosh, from the night of the train accident, regretted returning home.

Ashima at one point decides to stand up for herself and tried to adapt herself to the new land. Gradually, things become easier for her, yet the past memories were strong enough to cast a deep impact on her life. She chooses to retain the 'Indianness' in her. She did not touch beef, wore clothes other than sarees, cut off her hair or forgot her family in India or their values. In fact, she taught Bengali rituals, and she guides to cook Bengali foods to the newcomers from India. She tried to inculcate the same nationalistic zeal in her children. This led her to teach Gogol children's poem by Tagore and familiarize him with deities like Durga, Saraswati, Lakshmi, etc. But also being aware of the need of English in the land she lets him watch English shows like *Sesame Street, The Electric Company,* etc.

The family took the opportunity to visit Kolkata after every few years. Both husband and wife displayed a wider smile from such visits. Gogol and Sonia noticed how their parent turns "less complicated versions of themselves" (81). They were given a warm welcome and they brought them gifts of different items from America. This was the happiest moment for Ashima. She gets an opportunity to relive her past as she shops in New Market, goes to movies and accompanies her old school friends. It was a freedom for her. She "wanders" freely around the city" (83). Once such trips gets over, she relapse into silence and sadness. To her, it feels strange to return back to her cold and empty home that she has built with Ashoke in America. So, "Though they are home they are disconcerted by the space, by the uncompromising silence that surrounds them" (87).

Sometimes, their former home in Kolkata feels strange to them. Their few weeks pass like a dream to them. On the home, on Pemberton Road they feel as if they are the only Gangulis in the world. This shows the fading significance of their hundreds of relatives they had just visited in Kolkata. Eventually, their wish to claim their belongingness to the past seems impossible.

The family attempts to adapt themselves to the alien land and considers themselves as any other native families except for the name of Ganguli on the mailbox and their order of *India Abroad* and *Sangbad Bichitra* (64). For the sake of the children, they planted Christmas trees, they learned to roast turkey, celebrated thanks giving, Easter, and the birth of Christ. Ashima allows Gogol to consume edibles like cheese, mayonnaise, tuna fish, hot dogs etc. she made sandwiches with roast beef for Gogol. Yet, something always holds them back in their entire attempt to adopt the new culture and food habits.

In order to impart Indian values and knowledge the children were taken to Cambridge to see Apu Trilogy plays, or a Kathakali dance performance or a Sitar recital at Memorial Hall. Gogol is admitted to a class where every other Saturday he is taught Bengali language, culture, and also taught about his ancestral alphabet. He was acquainted to Bengali Renaissance and the revolutionary activities of Subhas Chandra Bose. His parents were aware of his English accents that sound exactly like the Americans. They were afraid of the fact that their son might not retain Indian culture, or he may become totally Americanised.

Occasions like birthday, or Saturday evening parties provided opportunities to the minority community for a get together to share their Indian sentiments. They often prepared Indian dishes like "Channa dal", "pineapple chutney", "sendeshes", "lamb curries", etc. for such occasions (72). Further, the womenfolk find their chance to dress in their best dazzling saris. While the man folk talks about affairs back in their homeland. They brought their children along with them as they do not believe in baby-sitters and also to make them learn and get connected to each other in the foreign land. Although they sometimes don't like each other much but it was because of the shared past that they mostly made Bengali friends.

Things grew more complicated for Ashima when her children were grown-ups. They had to part their ways from Ashima to pursue education. She was extremely miserable when Gogol one day addressed New Haven as his home by mistake. The value she attributes to a home was incomprehensible to Gogol. She angrily remarked how she has not considered America and her little home on Pemberton Road as 'home' even after living there for so many years. While her son, leaving in the suite only for three months has started calling it a home. For Ashima, home can only be in India because it is the land of freedom and belongingness. So, this shows how different characters have different views of home.

As a mother, she felt bad that her son lives in a dilapidated small apartment with little salary in New York and so provides him allowances. When she knew about his affair with Maxine, she showed her tolerance. As a loving mother, she approves of his plan to go on a vacation but demands his visit home with the girl. In the bottom of her heart, she was unwilling to accept her as a daughter-in-law. She did not like the English way of Maxine calling them by their name.

A turning point for Ashima came when she chooses to stay back in Massachusetts after her husband left for Ohio. This shows that she prefers her comfort zone to the new surroundings, where she would have nothing to do and moreover her husband would be busy with his research work. Once again, she was left alone the way she had her beginning in America. This decision has its benefit as it made her ready for the future circumstances.

She took up the task of making Christmas cards for the remaining three members of the family. This was her way of passing her loneliness. She was contended that she has made many friends in America, and she was easily understood by the store owner and was treated like any other customers. Her making of Christmas cards shows her willingness to accept the "other" culture on the one hand, and on the other she was aware of the engravings and scenes on such cards. She always preferred a card that reads, "Happy Holidays" or "Season's Greetings" instead of, "Merry Christmas" (160). Her rejection of the feature of nativity on English Christmas cards shows her attempt to invert the foreign culture and instead engrave the elephant symbol. This indicates her willingness to retain the

Indian image. The elephant is the reminder of her father who used to draw elephants for Gogol when he was small. This also shows her creation of hybrid stuffs. Once a year, she read the letters of her parents through which she tries to keep intact with them. So, "She revisits their affection and concern, conveyed weekly, faithfully, across continents—all the bits of news that had had nothing to do with her life in Cambridge but which had sustained her in those days nevertheless" (160-61).

Unlike her husband, son and daughter it was uneasy for her to accept a life of solitude at the age of forty-eight. There was nobody to talk to, entertain or cook for. She did not like the fact that she has to return in the evening to an empty home from the library. At night, she was afraid to be home alone in spite of the security system. So, she took up a job in the public library to pass the time, and she has made friends with other women at the library. They made her understand that at one point of time parents should not expect from their children to spend holidays with them. As she has also moved away from her own parents indicating her independence so she should also be willing to give them their independence. This shows her attempt to adjust to her life in late forties. Her husband spoke to her every night but that too soon stop as he called one night informing her that he is in the hospital due to stomach ache, and this proves to be his last call to her. He died suddenly of a massive heart attack. People shaken by the news of his death were distressed by how death had been unfair on the people who had given up everything to be in the foreign land to have for a better life.

Ashima no longer desired to escape to Kolkata. She disliked the idea, when her friends suggested her because she does not like to get away from the land that carries the memories of her husband. As a responsible mother, she realized her duty of her children's marriage that needed to be performed. She arranges and forces Gogol to see Moushumi Mazoomdar, as she is a Bengali girl. She was happy when saw her son settled down with a Bengali girl. However, she was unaware of the future that would befall on the couple.

Years after this, she throws a farewell party before leaving for India selling her house on the Pemberton road. Once again, she prepared an elaborate meal for her guests. She is leaving the house in which she has lived for the past twenty-seven years for a blurry home and identity. She wants to escape from there. She knew the American family, who bought the house, would renovate and change the structure of the house altogether. She carefully tries to capture it the way she has set it up and wish secretly that it would remain the way it was. As once decided, she was executing her past plan with her husband about the future to spend six months of the year in India and six months in America. To her, to be constantly in a foreign land is like a lifelong pregnancy. But remarkably, it is her home which she made with her husband. Nevertheless, it is crumbling down bit by bit. This thought terrifies her and made her lonely. She realize, she is the one with an American passport and thus not fully an Indian. So her dream to establish a home was fading, and thus she oscillates between two worlds.

As a child, Gogol shares the author's insecurities about his identity. Being born into Bengal immigrant families, they had to bear their parents' wish to imbibe in them the Bengali culture. He is forced to miss his art class on Saturdays in order to attend his Bengali lessons. He senses his "otherness" from an early age. Like other kids, he is not allowed to play the ballet or the softballs on Saturdays. He was 'in-between' the acquired culture from outside world and the one imparted to him by his parents. He was stuck between two cultures, two nations and two languages, and thus it becomes difficult to define his identity. He could not completely "mimic" the white ideals, nor could he disobey his Indian identity. Therefore, he turns out to be a 'hybrid' version of himself. Like Lahiri, he tried to adapt to both world as he attains maturity. Humorously, boys like Gogol were referred to as "ABCD: American-born confused Desi" (118).

As a kid, he feels sick that he is dragged to parties where there are full of his parents' Bengali friends and their children. He prefers American food more than Indian. Surprisingly, he felt a strange connection with the ancient Puritan spirits than the Bengali Renaissance flag bearers. The frequent visit to India does not excite him the way it does to his parents and their relatives in Kolkata. He knows the rows of relatives waiting for them at the airport but he did not feel connected to them. So, little he felt the sense of belongingness to India or its culture.

This was the reason he did not like his name "Gogol" when he grew up. Like other boys, he could not shorten it as it was catchy. He shared the same feeling of anguish with Lahiri, the author, by their 'pet name turned good name' (59). The author, Nilanjana Sudeshna is better known by her "convenient" pet name Jhumpa Lahiri. Gogol's name was a drawback for him. According to him, it does not define his true self and is painful to be Gogol. He did not realize that at Kinder Garden he himself loved the pet name "Gogol" and so the principal of the school registered him thus. His is good name "Nikhil" sounded strange to him. When he grew up with Gogol, he felt angry as his friends' teases him "Giggle" or "Gargle". Although on his fourteenth birthday his father had gifted him *The Short Stories of Nikolai Gogol*, he never bothered to open it until late in his life he will be inspired to read the works of Nikolai. He had to explain people the meaning of his name that it means nothing "Indian". He saw his name as absurd and obscure and due to this he does not date any girls like other boys of his age. The urge in him to change his name came when he studied a lesson on Nikolai Gogol, the Russian writer, on whom his name was kept. He was shocked and ashamed to learn about the biography of the Russian author. It detailed how he was never happy, had led a miserable life and was never married. That very night he complaint his parents regarding his name not knowing the actual reason behind naming him Gogol. Soon he was instigated to change his name giving examples of all those great personalities who had changed their name when they grew up. Unwillingly, his father waiting for the right time to reveal the secret behind naming him gave his consent for the name change.

An immense sense of freedom washed him after changing his name. He was no longer Gogol whose life was under the full clutch of his parents. It was a step taken by him to achieve his autonomy. He convinced his parents that "Nikhil", his new name, not only has a resemblance with Nikolai but it was a Bengali name meaning, "one who is entire, encompassing all" (56). As Nikhil, things became easier for him. He delved into a new personality. It is only as Nikhil he started making a carefree life for himself. He got his first girlfriend as Nikhil. He was romantically involved with a girl. It was possible to develop an intimate relationship with Ruth, his girlfriend, only as Nikhil. However, it did not last long.

He exercised another level of autonomy when he was admitted into a college in New Haven. He was very excited to be with his roommates there. Away from home, he found a free 'space' for himself. This by chance led him to address his suite as "home" to his mother, after which he had to bear her sentiments. But this is what he carries in his heart, as the suite provides him the freedom and comfort that a home generally gives. So, it was easy for him to call it his home. His regular visits to home on every weekend grew tiresome for him and moreover it takes away his little freedom. He felt the air heavy in the presence of his father, mother and Sonia in home.

Another form of escape came to Gogol when he moved further away to New York to a small and dark apartment in search of freedom. He did not care his parents' wish to stay in Massachusetts near them. Instead, he took up a small job in a farm as an architect. This also shows his constant attempt to search a free space for himself.

It is here that he met Maxine with whom he shares most of his time in New York. He was mesmerized by seeing Maxine's two storied mansion. He rejected his small apartment and was easily adapting into her luxurious home and lifestyle. He was fascinated to the free and gratifying life led by Maxine. He love the fact that he could come and go as he pleases in this home. It is appealing to him that the family is though generous; they would not go out of the way like his parents to accommodate others. In fact, he extremely idealizes the life of Maxine's father Gerald and Mother Lydia. It seemed to him as the cutest thing in the world to show off their love to each other. He felt the relationship that his father and mother had is ordinary and boring. So, he tries to mimic Gerald and Lydia's way of life and thought love marriage to be important.

The space along with the landscape at Ratliffs vacation home, in New Hemisphere, is something enchanting to him. Away from the world in the midst of desert and the sea without a medium of communication seemed a perfect place to him. This he thought to be his 'third space'. Far away from his parents he no longer feels the pressure to be loyal to their values. The urge in him to get into this world was so much so that he confesses his parents that he is seeing a girl when he was called back home to celebrate his birthday and see off his father for Ohio. He knew his parents would not like the fact that their only son loves an American girl but he was ready to hurt them.

When he celebrated his birthday in the farm house, among dozens of guest that Gerald and Lydia invited for the occasion, a lack of sense of belongingness strikes him. A woman attending the party inquired about his Indian heritage. She holds the view that India is a disease filled country and an outsider might catch it easily. But Nikhil, according to her, belonging to Indian origin does not have the danger of it. At this, Nikhil was disappointed as he sees himself more as an American. However, he is sad that he cannot escape his Indian roots. Thus, he is 'in-between', as he is confused between the two identities.

This freedom and space suddenly seemed captivity, and he felt suffocated after the news of the unfortunate death of his father. He terribly missed his father and felt guilty for being far away from home. Home, on Pemberton Road, was pulling him back, yet he was afraid to face the absence of his father. Suddenly, he felt a deep connection with his father when he remembered the fine day spent with him. His father, disobeying his mother, took him across the end of the sea, away from the hustle and bustle of the world to the peaceful and isolated place and asks him to remember the day forever.

Another subdued guilt evolve in him was his name change. He was upset the moment his father reveals the secret for naming him "Gogol". His father was compelled to tell him the story behind because Gogol's train was late that day due to some minor accident. Ashoke's heart pondered with worries as he was reminded of the terrible night when he had a train accident while he was travelling to Jamshedpur to his grandfather's house. It was a page from Nikolai Gogol's book that felt from his hand when he was lying half dead. The rescuer team saw it and he was led to the hospital. So, it is a kind of tribute that he pays to the genius Russian writer for saving his life, he named his son "Gogol". Now that Gogol has disrespected his father's honour, he felt extremely guilty of it. He drew back to silence and loneliness resulting in his beak up with Maxine. He detested the plan that Maxine made for the New Year's Eve to spend it at the vacation home in New Hemisphere. She tried to convince him that it will be good for him to escape from all this. Gogol was enraged to hear the idea and cut her sharply that he want to be part of it rather than searching for an escape. This indicates his returning back to home and its ideals.

He imagines how it might have affected his father and mother at the death of their grandparents. As a child, he laughed and was ashamed of the sight of his parents' tears. It's comprehensible to him how the sense of guilt for being far away from their grandparents might strike his parents. The people in India whom he thought to have little connection with his parents' life were now acquiring value. He could feel the pain of his parents at the death of their kin. This emotions and sensibility brings him closer to Indian heritage and thus cultivates the Indian spirit in him.

Gogol did not know that his father came to America to forget the accident and its aftermath. His father Ashoke was scared to remember how most of his body parts got damaged and kept him bed ridden for several months. It also slightly left him limp forever. Ashoke remembered Mr. Ghosh, from the train, who advised him to see and experience the foreign land as it would prove bliss to him. In order to come out of the trauma of the suffering, the sleepless nights, after the accident he finally decided to escape to America. When he was blessed a son there, he found it a way to pay back Gogol for his life. After naming his son the nights no longer haunted him instead it uplifted him at the thought of the present peaceful life that he exhibited in America. Thus for Ashoke too it was a kind of escape from his scary homeland experiences, so he efforts to own a home in America.

His daughter Sonia, although follows the American trend extensively, proves herself more valuable by being a devoted daughter. She shows herself as a responsible daughter who was there for her mother in the difficult times. She moved back home to be with her and travelled to workplace from there. Also, she chooses for herself a boy approved by her mother although he is an American. This shows her adaptability to both the cultures.

At the request of his mother Gogol obeys to meet, the Bengali girl, Moushumi Mazoomdar. He quickly fell in love with her and they were married within a year. Both were happy initially, but soon it ended as they tried to seek their individual space. Moushumi wanted to retain her freedom even after her marriage. She did not consider her marriage when once again she met her crush, Dimitri, an unmarried middle-aged professor. She was disloyal to her husband Gogol. It can be said that she did not idealize the marriage of her own parents' or other Bengalis. Instead, she looks up, the American couple, her friends whose way of living and values are quite different from theirs. She was a rebel who dislikes her roots and traditions, and she had the desire to escape from it. She expressed how she hated Bengali boys except Gogol. Her idea of freedom took her to Paris. It was only there where she got comfort. She kept searching for a third home. The first home being her parents' house curtailed her independence; her second home that she made up with Gogol was also a failure. Thus, she hunts for a third home as she has decided to move back to Paris after the divorce.

It can be concluded that, Gogol was also left with a no place that he can call home. He could not return to his parents' home, but he tried to establish his second home with Moushumi which again shambles down after their failed marriage. When for the last time he visited home to his mother's farewell party, he suddenly felt miserable as he was losing the sense of belongingness. The home where he grew up was crumbling down before his eyes. The same house will no longer exist to bring back his memories with his father, mother and Sonia. What draws his attention more was the untouched book of Nikolai Gogol that his father has gifted him for his fourteenth birthday. He was blessed to discover the book, amidst heaps of less important books, at the last moment. Now he has the desire to read the book with the same spirit with which his father had once gifted him. This indirectly would connect him to his father and through his father to the home where they lived together by virtue of Indian values.

Whereas for Ashima the home in Kolkata would not be the same, as she cannot get back to it completely. Her past life spent with her husband in America would keep on haunting her. While getting back to America, she would not find her home that once she set up with Ashoke. So, she must dive back true "...to the meaning of her name, she will be without borders, without a home of her own, a resident everywhere and nowhere" (276). For Ashoke Kolkata remained a mysterious place. He had the full urge to get back to his homeland, yet the idea equally repelled him when he was reminded of his past experiences. Escaping to this part of the world, it seems to them that "Even those family members who continue to live [in Kolkata] seem dead somehow, always invisible, impossible to touch" (65). Moushumi's search for a third home took her to Paris. She failed in her efforts to retain the kind of life that her parents or any Bengali family lived. Whether she likes it or not she cannot shake off her Indian origin, so she oscillates between the inherited world on the one hand and desired world on the other. Thus Lahiri, although considers herself as an American has high regard for her Indian roots. She has infused this dualism into her characters and made it an interesting read. She has time and again brought up the experiences of such individuals who had to adapt themselves in between two cultures, two nations and two languages. In an attempt to do so they often cross paths with loss of identity and brings in the questions of belonging, in-between, space, freedom, mimicry and hybridity.

References

Bhabha, Homi. "The Third Space". *Identity, Community, Culture.* Edited by Jonathan Rutherford, Lawrence and Wishart, 1990.

——. *The Location of Cultural*. Routledge, 1995.

Goonewardena, Kanishka, Stefan Kipfer, et al. (Eds.). *Space, Difference, and Everyday Life: Reading Henri Lefebvre*. Routledge, 2008.

Hooks, Bell. *Yearning: Race, Gender and Cultural Politics*. MA: South End Press, 1990.

——. *Bone Black: Memories of Girlhood*. Henry Holt and Company, 1996.

——. *Belonging: A Culture of Place*. Routledge, 2008.

Lahiri, Jhumpa. *The Namesake*. Harper Collins, 2007.

Lefebvre, Henry. *The Production of Space*. Blackwell Publishing, 1991.

Rushdie, Salman. *Imaginary Homelands: Essays and Criticism*. Granta Books, 1992.

Waugh, Patricia (Ed.). *Literary Theory and Criticism*. Oxford University Press, 2006.

www.merriam-webster.com

12

Dynamics of the Kamatapuri Movement

Manash Pratim Nath

Contemporary imagination often finds itself beset by deeds so profound that it impels a re-arrangement of relationships within the societal and hierarchal structures. Acts so far removed in time and space and yet they find resonance through generations. But, what defines these deeds, the markers in the temporal and spatial frame in historicity? Would Lachit Borphukan nobility and courage then suffice the definition of such quintessential action? Or could one consider the story of the king of Paundra, who had supposedly fled to settle in the banks of the river Karotoya, and in the process lost his identity? Deeds of unequal magnitude, yet their reverberations have been felt through time. These actions prefigure the myths and legends; they make for the 'historical consciousnesses' of a people retroactively directing the movements of the community—they decide the value systems through which meanings and relationships are construed in a wider public space. It is not my intention to go into what constitutes these deeds, rather, through this essay, I would like to understand how certain myths and legends that surround these actions have come to figure prominently in the Kamatapur Movement during the different phases of the movement through the twentieth century in successive acts of condonement and rejection. The Kamatapur Movement, as an ethno-nationalist movement, has also at times been at loggerheads with its neighbouring language movements vis-a-vis the Assamese language movement. It is also the objective of this paper to understand this conflict and try delineate the edges of these conflicting aspirations.

The narratives in historicity are but functions of larger societal functions, in what has been termed as a 'focus on the complex temporal nexus of past-present-future' (Hirsch and Stewart, 2005). Hirsch and Stewart were of the view that contemporary events were largely responsible for the associations drawn from the past. They iterate—

> Reconfiguring "historicity" to index the fuller qualities of this social and personal relationship to the past and future makes it a complex social and performative condition, rather than an objectively determinable aspect of historical descriptions. (Hirsch and Stewart, 2005, p. 262)

"Historicity" then is described as a human condition in flux, 'where versions of the past and future assume present form in relation to events, political needs, available cultural forms and emotional dispositions' (Hirsch and Stewart, 2005). This is significant in the context of the Kamatapur sub-nationalist movement as a certain dichotomy comes into play when we study the historicity of the movement over the 20th century—one that shifted from an identity based campaign to a language based movement.

The Koch-Rajbanshi community is said to be largely concentrated in the northern parts of West Bengal and western Assam in India, though we do find a sizeable population in northwest Bangladesh, and the Jhapa and Morang Districts of Nepal. A section of this population claims to be the descendants of the Kamarupa king Vishwa Singha and have come to identify themselves as Rajbanshis (Wilson and Bashir, 2016). To this effect, Wilson and Bashir write—

> Vishwa Singha (r. 1515–1540) was a Koch warrior king of the sixteenth-century kingdom of Kamarupa. Devised by Brahmin priests, a Kshatriya (warrior caste) ancestry was asserted for Vishwa Singha. Thereafter, new converts forewent the appellation Koch and adopted the new title of Rajbanshi or Sivbansi, the

> latter based on a mythical marriage between the Lord Siva and Hira, the human mother of Vishwa Singha. Since the king styled himself as Kshatriya, present-day descendants persist in their claims to superior status in the caste system, despite lack of consensus on this issue among Hindu priests, or members of the community. (Wilson and Bashir, 2016, p. 458)

The Rajbanshi Kshatriya movement started with the publication of the Indian Census Report of 1882, where the Rajbanshis were categorized with the Koch as belonging to the same tribe. This was vehemently opposed by the Rajbanshis who considered the Koch as being inferior to them. Rajib Nandi cites a letter written in February, 1891, by the president of Rangpur Religious order, Mahamohopadhyay Panditraj Yadaveshwar Tarkaratna, to the magistrate of Rangpur, F.A. Skyne, in response to his request for a comment on the petition filed by the Order. Panditraj Tarkaratna argues that the two 'jatis' were different and that the Rajbanshis had degraded to a lower order since they stopped practicing their sacred-thread wearing rites and other prescribed rituals. They claimed to be the descendants of the 'Raja'[1] and contended that they atleast be considered to be of the 'Vratya Kshatriya'[2] caste order. Though, the irony is not lost on us that these groups who were struggling to *find* themselves within the Varna structure and had to rely heavily on the Hindu scriptures and pundits to trace their ancestry, the final act of legitimacy was eventually to be derived from the British colonial government.

Thus, the newly formed 'Kshatriya Samity'[3] would go on to actively engage with the Brahmin pundits from Mithila and Nabadwip to help *ascertain* their ancestry and heritage as Kshatriyas (Nandi, 2014). In the process a new narrative was adopted. Nandi writes—

> The most popular version at that time goes like this: Rajbanshis had been the royal descendants of king of Paundra (a neighbouring country) who ran away and settled along the banks of Karotoya River in fear of Mahapadma Nanda, the Buddhist king of Magadha, because Nanda had vowed to annihilate all Kshatriyas from the world. Apprehending total elimination they

> hid their Kshatriya identity. Moreover, in absence of any interaction with Brahmins and other Brahminical castes, they slowly ceased to practise Kshatriya rituals and traditions and became "Vartya Kshatriya" in the process losing their Kshatriya identity and status. (Nandi, 2014, p. 581).

Consequently, the colonial government relented and the Census of 1911 did accommodate the new narrative - the Rajbanshis were held to be separate from the Koch. This amidst several claims that the Rajbanshis were Hinduized Koch of a semi-Mongoloid origin; though the Rajbanshis themselves refuted any such distinction (Nandi, 2014).

The need to be inducted within the Varna system was seen as a political necessity for the Rajbanshi. Nandi contends that the movement was not only an initiative for upliftment, it also carved out a distinction between them as superior, and the Koch as the inferior.

The second half of the 1920's saw a major shift in the nationalist narrative. In 1926-1927, the Kshatriya Samity began rallying behind Dr. B.R. Ambedkar in an apparent bid to be enlisted as "Scheduled Caste". Thereafter the socio-ethno narrative of caste supremacy was abandoned in favour of what Nandi terms as "Dalit identity", perhaps in retaliation to the indifference of the Bengali higher caste. The 'indigenous tribesmen' were also critical of the higher caste 'jotedars' and felt marginalized in their *own* lands[4] (Nandi, 2014). In what could earlier be termed solely as a caste movement, was slowly taking the form of an socio economic movement driven by a more visible insider-outsider debate. Wilson and Bashir remark—

> Fundamental to reformist movements were hidden economic, social and political issues that shaped Rajbanshi communities and influenced Rajbanshi identity formation. For example, Das Gupta (1992) describes deteriorating relations between jotedars and adhiars during the colonial period in Jalpaiguri District, which ultimately resulted in alienation of autochthonous lower economic classes (including the Rajbanshi) and

> led to the development of localized political networks. (Wilson and Bashir, 2016, p. 463)

Yet another dimension to this narrative was added when, on the 28th of August, 1949, Maharaja Jagaddipendra Narayan Bhupbahadur of Koch Bihar ceded his territories to the Union of India. Thereafter it was put under the charge of a Chief Commissioner appointed by the Government of India and later was converted into a district of West Bengal by the Cooch Behar (Assimilation of State Laws) Act in 1950[5] (Mandal, 2015). The partition had also resulted in a large displaced population and the subsequent influx from Bangladesh added to the fear of the community being marginalized. In what can only be considered a stark detour from its previous stand in the early parts of the 20th century, the Rajbanshi increasingly began identifying themselves as Koch-Rajbanshis. As Nandi aptly puts it, the narrative had changed from a Kshatriya birth right to that of *karma*—the Koch Rajbanshis would claim *Kshatriya*-hood by virtue of their deeds (Nandi, 2014). This act of constituting an alternate identity finds resonance in Eric Hobsbawm when he describes the idea of 'invented traditions'. He writes—

> The use of ancient materials to construct invented traditions of a novel type for quite novel purposes. A large store of such materials is accumulated in the past of any society, and an elaborate language of symbolic practice and communication is always available. Sometimes new traditions could be readily grafted on old ones, sometimes they could be devised by borrowing from the well-supplied warehouse of official ritual, symbolism and moral exhortation-religion and princely pomp, folklore and freemasonry. (Hobsbawm, 1983, p. 6)

The visible shift in ideology can be gauzed by Mandal's observation when he states that the terms 'Rajbanshi' and 'Kamatapuri' are not interchangeable. Rajbanshi is an ethnic community while 'Kamatapuri' meant association with the Kamatapur movement which was a 'political position' based on the language. Mandal notes that the rural spaces were mostly dominated by Bengali and Rajbanshi speakers. But he makes a distinction here—the language the Rajbanshi speak are not exclusive to the community alone. The language is spoken in variation by the majority of the rural population—'a political construct' to differentiate between the Bengali speakers, who claim the high culture and a *consortium* of ethnic groups who speak the Kamatapuri language and have been, through various political and socio-economic acts, relegated to a 'low culture' (Mandal, 2015).

The region may be suitably described as cauldron of fomenting nationalistic tendencies made possible within a space that may, at best, be termed as a frontier. The region's history and ethnicity cannot simply be termed as that of any one group. As Sanjib Baruah states with incredulity—the earliest books written in Assamese were under the patronage of the kings of Kamatapur, some fourteen miles south west of Koch Behar. Citing Banikanta Kakati, he goes on argue that the language spoken in north Bengal and western Assam (undivided Kamrup and Goalpara) had come from the same dialect group—the Rajbanshi dialect spoken in parts of North Bengal, Goalpara in Assam and Rangpur in Bangladesh, have close affinity with the Kamrupi dialect (Baruah, 1995).

Though Baruah contends that the semantic resemblance in such spaces was probably due to multilinguistic nature of the region, he makes his point of departure by arguing that 'dialects are independent of literary speech'[6]. Language, he states, is simply the dialect of a people with an army. Samrat (in a newspaper article which ironically is titled as 'Kamrupi: a language with no army') quotes linguist Suniti Kumar Chatterjee to allude to the shared ancestry of these languages—Magadhi Apabhramsa—from which emerged Bengali, Assamese, Oriya, Magahi, Maithili and Bhojpuriya. He further writes—

> The confusion of tongues of Lower Assam with Bengali dialects is perhaps not surprising since they share a common origin. Their ancestor is Kamrupi. Going further back, Bengali, Assamese, Odia, Bhojpuri, Magadhi and Maithili all originate from a language called Magadhi Apabhramsa—probably the language that was spoken, with some variations, in both Kamrup

> and what Hiuen Tsang called mid-India around 1,400 years ago. (Samrat, 2017)

Another poignant point that Samrat makes is the disdain for Bengali in Assam. Any association with Bengali, he explains is 'a risky matter in Assam'. The politics of the region has, to an extent, been shaped by its repulsion for the 'foreigner' Bengali. Since the dialects of Goalpara, Dhubri, among other lower Assam districts, are perceived to be Bengali, they are looked down upon. Further, he states, because of the intonation of the spoken languages they are sometimes mistaken for 'tongues from Bangladesh'. He uses the term 'dhekeri' to group these languages (Samrat, 2017).

Incidently, the Kamatapuri sub-national movement, in its 'autochthonous' narrative has a similar tenet—its abhorance for the *bhatias* (immigrated Bengalis)—who they believe are responsible for the loss of livelihood opportunities and encroachment of land. The Kamtapuri and Assamese language movements do share certain similarities, apart from its mutual fear of the Bangladeshi immigrants. Mandal notes that *All Kamtapur Student's Union (AKSU),* which began functioning from the campus of North Bengal University, was modeled after the *All Assam Student's Union (AASU).* Similarly, *Kamtapur Liberation Organization (KLO)*, the militant branch of the Kamatapuri movement was fashioned after and is connected to organizations such as *United Liberation Front of Ahom (ULFA)*, the militant faction that sprung out of the Assam movement of the 1980's (Mandal, 2015).

The point of conflict between the two movements arise of their interest in what could (in simplified terms) be termed as 'common grounds'. The Kamatapuris have always claimed the Goalpara district of Assam as their own, while the ceding of territory by the Assam Government would signify weakness on the Assamese side.

Both, the Koch and the Rajbanshis, are separately registered as 'Scheduled Caste' in West Bengal, though they have yet to be accorded 'Scheduled Tribe' status, as its multiple factions have been demanding (Wilson and Bashir). On the 3rd of September,

2020, the Assam Legislative Assembly passed three bills—The Moran Autonomous Council Bill, 2020, The Motok Autonomous Council Bill, 2020, and The Kamatapur Autonomous Council Bill, 2020—to create autonomous councils for the Moran, Motok, and Koch-Rajbongshi communities (Sentinel Digital Desk, 2020). Further, on the 8th of January, 2019, the Union Cabinet approved the Constitution (Scheduled Tribes) Order (Amendment) Bill, 2019, which was then introduced in the Rajya Sabha on 9 January, 2019, by the Minister of Tribal Affairs, Jual Oram. This Bill seeks to grant Scheduled tribe status to fourty-one groups, of which six belong to Assam (the Koch Rajbanshis are one among them) (Sarmah and Hazarika, 2020).

Perhaps the animosity between the ruling national party in Assam and various pro-Assamese linguistic groups have created a 'breathing space' for such sub-nationalistic movements to nurture within the larger purview of Assamese nationalism. That these movements are dependent on the current political trends has been ascertained beyond doubt; the region still remains mired by a multiplicity of cultures and dialects and the trajectory these nationalistic movements shall take remains difficult to predict.

Notes

1. The Raja of Paundra.
2. Downtrodden Kshatriyas (due to the fact that they had given up on their sacred ritual practices and could not be considered at par with the practicing Kshatriyas).
3. Formed in 1910 under the leadership of Panchanan Barma.
4. The Koch-Rajbanshis identified themselves as the autochthonous inhabitants of the land.
5. In 1874 the district of Goalpara was withdrawn from Koch Behar and tagged with the new created Assam Valley Province by the British colonial government. (Source: http://goalparadistjudiciary.gov.in/history.htm)
6. Baruha quotes noted linguist Suniti Kumar Chatterjee.

References

Baruah, Sanjib. (1995). "Western Cultural Boundary of Assam". *Economic and Political Weekly*, Vol. 30, Issue No. 44, pp. 2783-84.

Hirsch, Eric and Stewart, Charles. (2005). "Introduction: Ethnographies of Historicity". *History and Anthropology*, Vol. 16, No. 3, pp. 261-24.

Hobsbawm, Eric. (1983). "Introduction: Invented Tradition". *The Invention of Tradition*. ed. Hobsbawm, Eric & Ranger, Terence. Cambridge: Cambridge University Press. pp. 1-14.

Mandal, Arijeet. (2015). "Little Rebellions: Demands, Transgressions, and Anomalies in the Kamtapur Struggle". *Sanglap: Journal of Literary and Cultural Inquiry*, Vol. 1, Issue 2, pp. 103-26.

Nandi, Rajib. (2014). "Spectacles of Ethnographic and Historical Imaginations: Kamatapur Movement and the Rajbanshi Quest to Rediscover their Past and Selves". *History and Anthropology*, Vol. 25, No. 5, pp. 571-91.

Samrat. (2017, October 23). Kamrupi: a language with no army. Mint. Retrieved from https://www.livemint.com/Leisure/kWEvwN3D2I3rWlpr1oDKmL/Kamrupi-a-language-with-no-army.html

Sarmah, Jayanta Krishna and Hazarika, Joyjit. (2020, April 04). "Politics of Scheduled Tribe Status in Assam". *Economic and Political Weekly*, Vol. 55, Issue No. 14, pp. 18-20.

Sentinel Digital Desk. (2020, September 03). Assam Assembly passes bill for the creation of 3 more Autonomous Councils. The Sentinel. Retrieved from https://www.sentinelassam.com/north-east-india-news/assam-news/assam-assembly-passes-bill-for-the-creation-of-3-more-autonomous-councils-499234

Wilson, Margot and Bashir, Kamran. (2016). "'King's inheritors': understanding the ethnic discourse on the Rajbanshi as an indigenous community". *Social Identities: Journal for the Study of Race, Nation and Culture*, Vol. 22, No. 5, pp. 455-70.